S O U T H - W E S T E R N

Microsoft® PhotoDraw 2000

Manual — Beginning Course

Mark Ciampa
Director of Academic Computing
Volunteer State Community College
Gallatin, Tennessee

South-Western
Computer Education
an Imprint of Course Technology
Thomson Learning™

Australia • Canada • Mexico • Singapore • Spain • United Kingdom • United States

ISBN: 0-538-72429-3

1 2 3 4 5 6 7 8 9 10 PC 09 08 07 06 05 04 03 02 01 00

Printed in the United States of America

ELECTRONIC MEDIA—LIMITED WARRANTY

South-Western Computer Education, an imprint of Course Technology, a division of Thomson Learning ("South-Western"), extends the following warranty to only the original customer:

Warranty Coverage

This warranty covers the media on which the South-Western software data are recorded. This limited warranty does not extend to the information contained on the media and in the accompanying book materials (the "software/data"). The media product is warranted against malfunction due to defective materials or construction. This warranty is void if the media is damaged by accident or unreasonable use, neglect, installation, improper service, or other causes not arising out of defects in material or construction.

Warranty Duration

The media product is warranted for a period of three months from the date of the original purchase by the customer.

Warranty Disclaimers

The following should be read and understood before purchasing and/or using the media:

A. Any implied warranties that arise out of this sale are limited in duration to the above three-month period. South-Western will not be liable for loss of use of the media or other incidental or consequential costs, expenses, or damages incurred by you, the consumer, or any other user. Furthermore, South-Western will not be liable for any claim of any kind whatsoever by any other party against the user of the Software/data.

B. South-Western does not warrant that the Software/data and the media will be free from error or will meet the specific requirements of the consumer. You, the consumer, assume complete responsibility for any decisions made or actions taken based on information obtained using the Software/data.

C. Any statements made concerning the utility of the Software/data are not to be construed as expressed or implied warranties.

D. South-Western makes no warranty, either expressed or implied, including but not limited to any implied warranty or merchantability and fitness for a particular purpose, regarding the Software/data and makes all Software/data available solely on an "as is" basis.

E. In no event will South-Western be liable to anyone for special collateral, incidental, or consequential damages in connection with or arising out of the purchase or use of the Software/data. The sole and exclusive liability of South-Western, regardless of the form of action, will not exceed the purchase price of the media.

F. Some states do not allow the exclusion of limitation of implied warranties or consequential damages, so the above limitations or exclusions may not apply to you in those states.

Further Disclaimers of Warranty

South-Western will extend no warranty where the software is used on a machine other than that designated on the software package.

Media Replacement

Provided that you, the customer have satisfactorily completed and returned a copy of the License Agreement, South-Western will replace, during the warranty period, any defective media at no charge. At South-Western's option, the defective media must be returned postage prepaid, along with proof of purchase date. Please contact the Technical Support Hotline as shown on the next page for return instructions before returning any defective media.

Legal Remedies

This warranty gives you specific legal rights, and you may also have other rights that vary from state to state.

TECHNICAL SUPPORT HOTLINE

Our support staff are available to answer your questions about our products and help with any technical problems. While we do not provide direct support to student users of our products, we are happy to help instructors and the staff of microcomputer labs. Please do not permit your students access to the hotline information.

If you identify a problem, please check your hardware to make sure it is working properly. If the hardware is functioning correctly, refer to the technical support hotline information below. Many software products include on-line help. If the answer is not available in the printed materials, try using the Help feature of the software. Please have the following information and materials with you when calling the hotline:

- Program, data, or Electronic Instructor CD-ROM
- Text
- Instructor's manual
- List of any error messages
- Student printouts
- Description of the problem
- Computer type and model
- Computer's memory configuration
- Version number of operating system
- Network version, if applicable
- Name and version number of commercial software, if applicable

If you are a high school, you can contact the Thomson Learning Technical Support Hotline at:

Phone: 800-543-0453
Available business hours (9 a.m. to 5 p.m. Eastern time) Monday through Friday
E-mail address: hotline.education@swpco.com
Fax: 800-880-9496
Product Information only: call 800-824-5179
Mailing Address: Technical Support
South-Western/Thomson Learning
5101 Madison Rd.
Cincinnati, OH 45227

If you are any school or institution other than a high school, you can contact the Course Technology Technical Support Hotline at:

Phone: 800-648-7450, ask for Technical Support
Available business hours (9 a.m. to 5 p.m. Eastern time) Monday through Friday
E-mail address: tech.support@course.com
Web: www.course.com, find the option for Support and Technical Support Request
Fax: 617-621-3078
Product Information only: call 800-648-7450, ask for Customer Service
Mailing Address: Technical Support
Course Technology/Thomson Learning
One Main St.
Cambridge, MA 02142

CONTENTS

PLANNING THE COURSE

PART A—LESSON PLANS

PART B—SOLUTIONS FOR REVIEW QUESTIONS

PART C—PRINTED OUTPUTS FROM STEP-BY-STEP EXERCISES AND PROJECTS

PLANNING THE COURSE

Objectives and Design of the Course

The primary objective of the course is to help participants learn to use Microsoft PhotoDraw. After completing the text, learners will have developed and practiced PhotoDraw processing skills and will be confident using these skills for personal, school, career, and/or business projects.

These learning materials are designed to be used either in an instructor-led or in a self-paced environment. If the materials are used in a self-paced environment, there should be a knowledgeable person nearby to help when learners press wrong keys or click the wrong part of the screen. Learners who have previous PhotoDraw experience and are familiar with Windows may be able to work through the book on their own without any help.

Completion Time

Estimated completion times are included for each lesson but will vary depending on each learner's previous computer experience. An average completion time to complete material in the text-workbook is 12+ hours.

System Requirements

Some PhotoDraw features are installed by default; others are installed on first use by default; and still others are only installed by doing a custom installation. If the book is to be used in a classroom, be sure features are installed before beginning the lesson.

To use PhotoDraw 2000 Version 2, you need:

- An IBM-compatible computer with a Pentium 166 or higher processor
- Windows 98, Windows 95, Windows 2000, or Windows NT Workstation 4.0 or later with Service Pack 2 or later
- A 3.5-inch floppy drive (optional)
- A CD-ROM drive
- At least 32 MB of memory
- A hard disk large enough to support all your applications and store learner material
- A VGA or better video display
- A mouse

General Teaching Suggestions

The suggestions here pertain to the whole course. Suggestions specific to each lesson appear in Part A of this manual.

The Book

As the instructor, you should work through the entire book before beginning instruction. That way you can feel confident that you know the various features available in PhotoDraw 2000.

Terminology

It is very important for your learners' success in using the PhotoDraw application that you use Microsoft's terminology for its various features and procedures. For example, if you refer to selecting as highlighting, learners will be at a disadvantage when they need to use the Help feature to get information about the procedure. All terminology from previous applications needs to be replaced with Microsoft's.

Projection Equipment

If the materials are used in an instructor-led classroom, it is very helpful to use some kind of projection equipment so you can point to various parts of the screen when teaching learners how to accomplish tasks.

Group Help

If you are teaching in an instructor-led environment, be sure to impress upon the learners that they should stay with you during class rather than get into difficulties that will take class time to remedy. Other learners often become very unhappy with those who go off on their own and then expect the class to wait while they get help.

You can make the classroom experience much more meaningful if you can find acceptable ways of using learners' difficulties with the application to instruct the entire class as problems occur. It is sometimes a good idea to have all learners look at the screen where the problem occurred.

You might begin a class by telling learners that you are not "picking on" anybody when you call attention to errors. It may help others avoid making the same mistakes or to find their way to solutions. It even helps to congratulate those who make errors from which others can learn.

Individual Help

When a learner has difficulties with a procedure and requests your help, be sure he or she is the one to correct the problem. You should never be the one to correct the problem by pressing the keys or using the mouse. Rather, explain what needs to be done, and let the learner do it.

You should stress the importance of a learner watching the screen to see and understand everything he or she is doing in the lesson.

When a number of learners have trouble with the same procedure, consider giving a brief instruction session to all participants. It will save time in the long run.

Features Not Covered in Class

If learners will not complete all the material in the book, it is important for you to detail for them the features of PhotoDraw that are available. Application users cannot use any application efficiently if they know only a few basic features, and then try to accomplish more complicated tasks, without knowing there are features that would make those tasks easy.

The word *basic* may be misleading as it pertains to a software application. What one might consider a very advanced feature might well be a basic feature as far as another individual's needs are concerned. Encourage learners who have needs you do not cover to use either the book itself or the Help command to find out how to use other features of PhotoDraw.

Screen, Solution, and Printout Variations

Because of differences in equipment, there may be variations between what is shown in illustrations in the book and what appears on the screens of learners' computers. This may be caused by variations in monitor configurations.

Printed output may also differ from sample solutions in the instructor's manual because of variations in the way printers handle fonts and learner discretionary choices in style elements.

Instructional Materials

This instructional package includes the text-workbook packaged with a CD-ROM and an electronic instructor CD-ROM packaged with this manual. Testing software is also available, which has a customizable test bank specific for the text.

Text-Workbook

The text-workbook is organized around the following features:

- Learning objectives at the beginning of each lesson give an overview of the lesson.
- Instructions for specific operations allow independent progress.
- Step-by-Step exercises immediately following the presentation of new concepts and instructions give the opportunity to apply what has just been learned.
- Marginal boxes provide additional information and activities.
- Screen captures explain complex concepts and serve as reference points.
- Review questions, projects, and critical thinking activities follow each lesson as a means to gauge understanding of the lesson's concepts and operations. The Critical Thinking Activity at the end of each lesson is provided for those who are moving at a faster pace and need a challenge.
- A glossary provides definitions of basic features encountered in learning about PhotoDraw.
- A comprehensive index supplies quick and easy accessibility to specific parts of the book.

Data CD-ROM

The data CD-ROM which is packaged with the text workbook contains data files that are used in Step-by-Step exercises and for projects. The data files may be copied for participants in classes; they allow learners to use time learning computer operations rather than keying data into the computer.

Each data files is named according to the Step-by-Step exercise or the project in which it is first used. A data file to be used in the exercise called Step-by-Step 4.3, for example, is named **Step-by-Step 4-3.** Learners are asked to save most files as they would any file they edit.

If you do not want learners writing over the data files, you can add read-only passwords to the files to prevent modification. You can then give learners instructions for renaming their documents when they save them. You can add a read-only password by choosing the Save As command on the File menu and then clicking the Tools menu drop-down button to display the General Options dialog box. Enter a password in the Password to Modify box.

The location of files is critical. Data files for the exercises and projects must be stored on a hard drive. It is important that learners not become accustomed to working from the floppy or CD-ROM drive when they use PhotoDraw 2000.

We suggest that you create a separate folder for each learner. You should copy the data files needed for the exercises in the book into each learner's folder. The learner can also save files as instructed to that folder.

To make it easy for learners to save often while working on their files, it is suggested that you direct them to save files to the same folder where their data files are located. To avoid running out of hard disk space, have learners move their completed exercise files—the renamed files—to floppy disks at the end of each class period.

Electronic Instructor CD-ROM

The Electronic Instructor CD-Rom packaged with this manual contains a wealth of teaching aids to help you prepare for your classes. Following is a list of the folders included on the Electronic Instructor:

- Career Worksheets
- Evaluation
- Individual Learning Strategies
- Internet Behavior Contract
- Instructor Lesson Plans
- Portfolio Guidelines
- SCANS Correlations
- Scheduling (including block scheduling)
- Solution Files
- Data Files
- Learner Lesson Plans
- Test Questions
- Transparency Graphics Files

LESSON PLANS

PART A

LESSON 1 *Introduction to PhotoDraw*

Teaching Materials

- Lesson 1 of the user textbook
- Online access to PhotoDraw Home Page
- Lesson 1 Test from *Electronic Instructor* CD-ROM

Prepare

- Introduce the new vocabulary for this lesson as presented in the *Vocabulary* list on the first page of the lesson.
- Explain that this lesson is a quick introduction to PhotoDraw and some of its basic features.
- Point out that the purpose of the sidebar items that are embedded within the text material throughout the lesson is to provide the learner with important background information. Boxed sidebar items occur under these three different headings throughout the book: *Note, Internet,* and *Hot Tip. Notes* is used to provide information about PhotoDraw and graphic design in general. The *Internet* gives facts and figures about its history, and its future in our society. The sidebar *Hot Tip* gives shortcuts and tips for using PhotoDraw.
- The class can access South-Western Educational Publishing's PhotoDraw Web site for additional information and links to important Web sites throughout the book.

Teach

There are two important introductory items to cover prior to "jumping in" to PhotoDraw. First, it is important that learners understand just what PhotoDraw is. Microsoft PhotoDraw 2000 Version 2 is a combination of several different applications. PhotoDraw is a graphics design program used to create graphic images for use on business cards, letterheads, flyers, and other printed documents. PhotoDraw is also a photographic editing program that can be used to touch-up or change a photograph and, in addition, it is an Internet Web design tool that can be used to create and edit graphics for Web sites. It would be advisable to have printed examples of business cards, letterheads, an original and touched-up photograph, and also to visit a Web site that has used PhotoDraw to create a graphic image. This helps learners better understand how PhotoDraw can be used.

The second important item to cover is vocabulary. PhotoDraw sometimes uses terms that are different from our normal vocabulary. For example, something created with PhotoDraw is called a picture. In our normal way of speaking, a picture can be something drawn or even a photograph.

Emphasize to learners that from the outset it's important to know the correct PhotoDraw vocabulary to prevent confusion later on.

The PhotoDraw Screen begins the discussion of the basic look and functions of PhotoDraw. It's important that learners understand the terms used in describing the screen layout (picture, workspace, background, scratch area, workpanes, picture list, etc.). It is also important that learners call a PhotoDraw creation a picture. Help learners understand that all pictures in PhotoDraw are made up of objects. You might illustrate this from a classroom: learners, chairs, chalk, and computers are all objects. It's easy to rearrange these items in the classroom when the objects are moved. (You might even have learners move to different seats temporarily.) Now have the learners try to rearrange the room without considering everything as an object. The ability to manipulate objects has many advantages.

The menu bar system in PhotoDraw is similar to other Microsoft Office applications. If your learners are familiar with Office you may have them launch Word, Excel, or Access and compare the menu system to that of PhotoDraw's. The exception is the Visual Toolbar, which is a combination of the menu bar and standard toolbar. PhotoDraw's Help system is identical to that of the other Office applications.

Step-By-Step 1.1 helps learners start using PhotoDraw, discover its screen layout, and use the toolbars. It also introduces learners to the Microsoft Help system.

The *Note* regarding the Visual Toolbar shows learners that this bar can be turned off if screen space is at a premium. The *Hot Tip* regarding the Formatting toolbar explains that, unlike other Office products, PhotoDraw does not have this toolbar on by default because its features are found in other PhotoDraw toolbars.

Enter and Save Text enables learners to create text objects and learn how to move them around on the background. Although objects can also be moved to the scratch area, this will be covered later. Occasionally learners have initial difficulty dragging items on the screen because they don't use the mouse properly. Remind them that a mouse should be moved with the palm of the hand and the fingers should naturally drape over the buttons. That way, when the mouse pointer is in the proper position, the fingers are also in the right position to click a button. The importance of saving cannot be overestimated. Now is a good time to help learners develop the habit of saving regularly, either when they complete a task or every 10 minutes. You might even ask learners for their own personal horror stories about when they or a friend did not save and lost a document or project. The mantra "save, save, save" should be ingrained in all learners. The Microsoft Image Extension (.MIX) format saves all of the PhotoDraw picture, including items on the scratch area. The other types of file formats will be discussed later.

The Step-By-Step 1.2 has the learner create three text objects and move them on the background. Placement of these objects is relative at this time; they can be moved again if necessary. Show learners where to save their pictures. If they are using a diskette, it would be advisable for everyone to format that diskette together. Many learners have encountered problems saving because they thought a disk was formatted! Have everyone do it together and avoid this problem.

The *Hot Tip* sidebar on using Ctrl + T explains a very handy (and often-used) shortcut when entering text objects. The *Note* about word wrap reminds learners that although this is a nice feature for word processing, it is not used in a graphics package like PhotoDraw.

Format Text focuses on changing the appearance of the text objects. Allow learners to scroll through the different font types to see the wide variety available in PhotoDraw (over 120) with Disc 2 inserted. You may even ask learners to create five text objects using five different font types and then decide when these should be used (and not used). For example, some font types would be suitable for a flyer advertising a sale while others would be inappropriate for publicizing a meeting. Remind learners that if a font type is bold by nature (like Arial Rounded MT Bold), then selecting bold as the style will have no effect.

The Picture Setup dialog box allows learners to specify the output: letter, envelope, mailing label, etc. This changes the background as well. Print Preview helps learners see just how a picture will look when it is printed. Encourage learners to use Print Preview regularly before printing (and printing and printing!) on paper.

Step-By-Step 1.3 has learners change the output size, dress up the text objects with different font types and point sizes, preview the picture, and save it.

The *Note* regarding point size describes this unit of measure. The *Hot Tip* about formatting text shows that the quick menus can be used as with all Office applications.

Apply Special Effects introduces a more advanced way to change the appearance of text objects. Designer Text offers over 50 combinations of attractive fonts with professionally selected borders with Disc 2 inserted. Bend Text does just that: it curves the text for an eye-catching appearance while 3-D adds that extra dimension (pun intended!) to grab attention. However, 3-D often requires the Rotate and Tilt option. This is a good opportunity for learners to experiment with all of these special effects. You may want to allow them time just to play with these different selections, to become comfortable with their use, and to see what is and is not effective.

Step-By-Step 1.4 applies these different special effects on text objects.

The *Internet* sidebar explains what "spam" is (some have defined it as "junk e-mail") and how common it has become. You may want to have learners do research regarding ways in which spam can be blocked. The *Internet* sidebar on Internet-accessible cities shows which US cities have the best Internet access.

Printing PhotoDraw Pictures explores the different print options. Of all of these options, the orientation (landscape and portrait) is one of the most important. You may want to print out a picture in both orientations to show the difference (or have the learners see this themselves with Print Preview).

Step-By-Step 1.5 prints the picture after using Print Preview.

The *Internet* sidebar about Internet shopping reveals that most learners still use the Internet to gain information about products instead of using it to purchase those products.

Close

Have learners complete the end-of-lesson *Vocabulary Review* and *Review Questions. Vocabulary Review* requires learners to provide written definitions for key terms from the lesson. The *Review Questions* test learners' understanding of lesson concepts, requiring them to think critically about ideas discussed in class.

Project 1-A has learners change the picture size to a #10 Envelope and create a return address and mailing address. Learners will need to use Print Preview in order to see if they have moved the text objects to the correct locations.

Project 1-B involves retrieving a file and changing the appearance of the text objects with different font styles and sizes. As a variation, you may want the learners to change all of the text objects in the picture with different font styles, font types, and sizes.

Project 1-C asks the learner to make a flyer more attractive with Bend Text, Designer Text, and 3-D Text. Learners will also change the other text objects to styles of their choosing.

Critical Thinking Activity has learners create a flyer and make it attractive. You may want to have different learners make suggestions about each other's choices of styles. This helps them begin to see what is attractive and what is not.

Assess

Assign the Lesson 1 Test located on the *Electronic Instructor* CD-ROM.

Vocabulary

object—An item like a photograph, image, or text in PhotoDraw

picture—A completed PhotoDraw design

workspace—The entire area used when creating a picture

background—The rectangle that appears in the center of the workspace

scratch area—The gray area that surrounds the background

workpanes—The area to the right of the background that displays the tools and options to perform a certain task.

picture list—The area located to the left of the workspace that shows small versions of the pictures that are currently open

active picture—The picture that is framed by a blue rectangle and is displayed on the workspace

visual toolbar—A combination of the menu bar and standard toolbar that displays related commands

text object—An object composed of words in a PhotoDraw picture

Designer Text—Predefined PhotoDraw special effect styles that are combinations of attractive fonts with professionally selected borders and colors

Bend Text—A PhotoDraw special effect that curves text

3-D—A PhotoDraw special effect that makes the text appear as if it is in a 3-dimensional format

Rotate and Tilt—A PhotoDraw feature that repositions a text object so both the faces of the letters and the depth can be shown

portrait—An orientation in which a picture is printed in the standard up-and-down format on paper

LESSON 2 *Using Templates and Wizards*

Teaching Materials

- Lesson 2 of the learner textbook
- Online access to PhotoDraw Home Page
- Lesson 2 Test from *Electronic Instructor* CD-ROM

Prepare

- Introduce the new vocabulary for this lesson as presented in the *Vocabulary* list on the first page of the lesson.
- Emphasize that this lesson introduces two key features of PhotoDraw that make it very easy to use: *templates* and *wizards.*
- Remind learners that the purpose of the sidebar items, embedded in the text of the lesson, is to provide important background information. Boxed sidebar items occur under these three different headings throughout the book: *Note, Internet,* and *Hot Tip.*
- The class can access South-Western Educational Publishing's PhotoDraw Web site for additional information and links to important Web sites throughout the book.

Teach

PhotoDraw is easy to use, as seen from the previous lesson, but there are still some levels of complexity that can make it difficult to create a finished picture. First, designing a picture with the right combination of font sizes and types, Designer Text, Bend Text, and graphics is something that comes with practice. Unless the learner has an especially critical eye, what looks attractive to him or her may not look so to the rest of the world. In addition, the necessary steps for printing on certain types of paper or transporting a PhotoDraw picture to Word or PowerPoint may take many steps that have to be done in a specific sequence. However, PhotoDraw includes two life-saving tools that make these tasks much easier to perform. Those tools are templates and wizards. Learners should understand that these tools, found in all Microsoft Office programs, will save time and will help to produce projects that are stunning. You may even find, if you take an informal survey, that several learners are already familiar with templates and wizards from other Office programs.

Again, it is important to emphasize the correct PhotoDraw vocabulary. PhotoDraw sometimes uses terms that differ from our normal vocabulary. Emphasize to learners that, from the outset, it's important to learn the correct PhotoDraw vocabulary to prevent confusion later.

Introduction to Templates begins with a definition of a template and a description of how to use one. A template is a predefined PhotoDraw picture that is easy to modify. It contains the right combination of fonts, colors, and other design features. You can easily customize the template by adding your own text objects or graphics. The advantage of using a template is that you do not have to create a picture from scratch. PhotoDraw has five sets of templates available.

It is important that learners feel comfortable navigating through all of the PhotoDraw templates. The first level of templates is called a category (Web Graphics, Cards, etc.). Each category has several subcategories. Within the subcategories are the actual templates themselves. If learners are to be productive in their use of templates, they will need time to experiment with moving through the levels of categories.

Step-By-Step 2.1 helps learners begin using PhotoDraw templates and moving through the categories and subcategories. There is no output for this Step-By-Step activity.

The *Note* about all Microsoft programs using templates is helpful when working with these programs. Instead of creating something from scratch, using a template can be a great time-saver. The *Internet* tip on the history of the Internet can help learners see how it evolved. The US Government was concerned how its military computers, in the midst of the Cold War, would be able to communicate with other computers, built by different manufacturers, and located across the country. ARPANET was designed and built to address these concerns. The *Hot Tip* about moving the template workpane is easily illustrated by having the learners do just that. There are occasions when moving this workpane to the opposite side of the screen may be helpful. For example, if you are working at the right edge of the screen, sometimes the workpane can encroach onto the workspace. Moving it to another location can eliminate this problem.

Using Card Templates gets learners started on designing a card from a template. PhotoDraw templates contain some step-by-step assistance in creating a finished template. There are four steps necessary to create a template. Be sure to walk through each of them with learners. Also, help learners to see that the text they enter and change is done in the template workpane, and then it is reflected in the workspace. It is important to point out that, in the last step of the process, you click on **Finish** and then you must save the picture. It is not automatically saved for you.

The Step-By-Step 2.2 has the learner create a greeting card from a template and change the text objects. If, for some reason, the fonts listed in the activity do not appear on your computer, just select another font style. This activity also asks students to be sure to center the text on the card. Again, let learners know where they should save their pictures.

The *Hot Tip* sidebar about moving an object is helpful when the object only has to be nudged slightly. Instead of using the mouse, a tap on the arrow key may be enough.

Create and Print Address Labels introduces learners to the powerful Print Reprint feature. This PhotoDraw life-saver makes it very easy to print output on gummed address labels and other special stock paper. PhotoDraw includes several popular paper, sticker, and label sheet sets, such as *Avery 8160—Address Label.* You may want to assign some learners to the task of identifying several of the more commonly used sets so they can tell the other learners when to select these types of paper. When using Print Reprint, the current picture will be automatically moved to the Picture List. This is a very powerful feature in PhotoDraw, and we will return to it later. For now, explain to learners that it is a holding area for their pictures.

Step-By-Step 2.3 has learners create a shipping label and print it on *Avery 8763—Shipping Label.* These will print on standard paper as well. Be aware that, for some of these sets, a printer with limited memory may cause an error message and only print part of the output. You may also want to remind learners that there is no Save feature for Print Reprints, as there is when creating a template. That's because Print Reprints is only producing output, not altering a picture.

The *Internet* tip regarding the proliferation of illegally copied software is eye opening. Learners often don't see the negative impact of copying software. The *Note* on how Print Reprints adjusts the size of the picture illustrates the convenience of this feature. Imagine the steps involved if, through trial and error, you had to make the adjustment yourself. The *Hot Tip* sidebar on using a picture not on the Picture List can save time. If you have already created and saved a picture, you do not have to open it and place it on the Picture List. Instead, click on the Browse button and locate that picture on your hard drive.

Working With Wizards introduces learners to the other important PhotoDraw tool, a wizard. Help learners understand the difference between a wizard and a template. Whereas a template presents you with a picture that you can customize, a wizard provides step-by-step help in performing an activity. A wizard asks a series of questions and then, based on your answers, it enables you to complete a project. However, there is some overlap in these two tools because a template does ask questions, though not as many as a wizard. One of the most powerful wizards in PhotoDraw is the Save For Use In wizard. This wizard helps you save your PhotoDraw picture so that it can be used on the Web or imported into another Microsoft Office program, such as a Word document or a PowerPoint presentation.

PhotoDraw templates and the Save For Use In wizard are often used together to create and import a background. You may wish to emphasize that this is where PhotoDraw's power begins to shine. Other products like Word or PowerPoint lack the capabilities of PhotoDraw to create colorful background images. However, they can easily be created in PhotoDraw and then imported into other Office programs. This also shows the tight integration between the family of Office programs. The Save For Use In wizard has several questions spread out over several screens. You may want to take the time to look at each question in some detail so that learners can see just what this wizard can do.

Step-By-Step 2.4 creates a background theme and imports it into PowerPoint. Note that this activity should only be done if PowerPoint is installed on that computer. If it is not installed, you can instead have learners save it to a file.

The *Internet* tip about the most active Web site demonstrates how powerful the Internet has become as a source for up-to-the-minute information. You may ask your learners to calculate the number of hits this site took each second (almost 4,000) and compare that with the hits taken on a favorite site of theirs in a 24-hour period.

Close

Have learners complete the end-of-lesson *Vocabulary Review* and *Review Questions. Vocabulary Review* requires learners to provide written definitions for key terms from the lesson. The *Review Questions* test learners' understanding of lesson concepts, requiring them to think critically about ideas discussed in class.

Project 2-A has learners create a postcard using a template. They also change font and point sizes accordingly.

Project 2-B involves retrieving the file created in Project 2-A and using Print Reprints to print it. The *Avery 3263 Postcard* will print four postcards to a page. Of course, this will also work with standard paper loaded into the printer.

Project 2-C asks the learner to retrieve a file that has a background and import it into PowerPoint. Again, be sure that PowerPoint is loaded on that computer. As an option, if learners are already familiar with PowerPoint, you can have them make a presentation using this background.

Critical Thinking Activity has learners create attractive tent cards. You may want to have different learners make suggestions about each other's choice of styles. This helps learners begin to see what is attractive and what is not. They also use Print Reprints to print the cards. *Avery 5305—Tent Card* prints two cards to a page.

Assess

Assign the Lesson 2 Test located on the *Electronic Instructor* CD-ROM.

Vocabulary

template—A predefined picture with the correct combination of text objects, colors, and other design features

tent card—A card that is folded in half and placed where someone is sitting to identify that person

Print Reprints—A PhotoDraw feature that has the ability to customize printing

Picture List—Displays thumbnails of all the pictures that are currently open in PhotoDraw

Wizard—Provides step-by-step help in performing an activity by asking a series of questions

Save For Use In—A wizard that helps save a PhotoDraw picture so that it can be used on the Web or in another Microsoft Office program

Importing—Transferring a picture or document to another program

Background—A PhotoDraw picture on which graphics or text can be displayed

LESSON 3 *Creating a Web Page*

Teaching Materials

- Lesson 3 of the learner textbook
- Online access to PhotoDraw Home Page
- Lesson 3 Test from *Electronic Instructor* CD-ROM

Prepare

- Introduce the new vocabulary for this lesson, as presented in the *Vocabulary* list on the first page of the lesson.
- Remind learners that the purpose of the sidebar items, embedded in the text of the lesson, is to provide important background information. Boxed sidebar items occur under these three headings throughout the book: *Note*, *Internet*, and *Hot Tip.*
- The class can access South-Western Educational Publishing's PhotoDraw Web site for additional information and links to other related Web sites.

Teach

Use PhotoDraw to create Web pages? is often the typical reaction when someone hears about working with this program to build Web pages. Usually we think of using Microsoft FrontPage or Word to construct a Web page. But these two programs are on opposite ends of the spectrum when it comes to Web page development. FrontPage and competing products like HotMetal represent the high end of Web development. They not only help you design and create a Web page but they are also used to maintain and administer entire Web sites. Microsoft Word, on the low end of the spectrum, can be used to create a basic Web page, but it is really just taking a Word document and saving it as HTML. PhotoDraw falls in the middle of these extremes. It can be used to create dazzling Web pages with sophisticated features like animated GIFs, rollovers, and other effects impossible to do in Word and, sometimes, even difficult to do in FrontPage. However, PhotoDraw handles them with ease. Although PhotoDraw lacks the capabilities to administer a Web site, it is as an excellent tool for creating Web pages that can then be imported into FrontPage.

Defining the Web page begins with a discussion of HTML and the different ways that you can create a Web page with it. You may want to have some basic HTML code available for learners to see. Walk them through the code and help them see the fundamentals of this basic language. You might also remind learners that HTML code is sent from the Internet to the browser on your computer. It's the browser's job to interpret the code and display it on your screen. The steps involved in creating a Web page with PhotoDraw are also discussed. There are three basic steps in creating a Web page with PhotoDraw:

1. Define the Web page.
2. Create the graphics and text.
3. Preview and save the page.

Defining the picture size is an important step in creating a Web page. The concept of a pixel is introduced here. Remind learners that anything on a computer screen, from text to the most detailed image, is entirely composed of individual dots (pixels). A good visual aid is a photograph from a newspaper. When examined closely, it's easy to see that this picture is made up of different colored (or shaded) dots. You may want to help learners understand the different resolutions of a monitor. In Windows 98, click on **Start | Settings | Control Panel | Display | Settings** to change the resolution. Most screen resolutions are set to 800 × 600 for creating Web pages. These can be set in PhotoDraw when the picture is first created or later through the Picture Setup dialog box.

A background is a very important effect on a Web page that is often overlooked. Encourage learners to surf the Internet and find a Web page that has no background and a similar page that does. The page that lacks a background looks plain while the page with a background immediately attracts your attention. Obviously the appearance of the background is critical.

A background in PhotoDraw can be created in one of two ways. First, you can use templates which are predefined backgrounds designed for Web sites. Creating a Web background template follows the same steps as using any PhotoDraw template. Step-By-Step 3.1 creates a background using a template and then changes the resolution to 800 × 600.

The second method of creating a background in PhotoDraw is to create one from scratch. PhotoDraw includes hundreds of pictures (called PhotoDraw content) for use in designing Web pages. When these pictures are used as background they are generally made transparent. Be sure that learners understand that a transparent picture is one that lets the background color "bleed" through; it is not just a faded picture. For a particular special effect, you can have a background of a specific color and make the picture transparent so that the background color bleeds through.

Step-By-Step 3.2 creates a background from scratch using PhotoDraw content. Learners may have some slight difficulty navigating PhotoDraw content folders for the first time. It helps to allow them time to explore the different folders and see all of the content available for use. As always, the PhotoDraw CD-ROM 2 must be in the CD-ROM drive or else its content must be loaded onto the hard drive.

The incredibly rapid growth of the Internet is illustrated in the *Internet* tip that shows how quickly the amount of Web traffic doubles as compared to telephone communication, even with its explosive use of cellular phones. You may want to ask learners to surf the Web and find more statistics about how quickly the Internet is growing. The *Internet* tip reveals that a thumbnail is really quite small in terms of pixels. Of course, the advantage is that it loads very quickly, while a large image may take much longer. You may want to have learners go online and time some sites that have very large images (they're easy to find!) and then time sites that only show thumbnails. A popular trick is to load only a thumbnail but have it hyperlinked to a much larger image. When someone moves the mouse over the thumbnail the pointer turns into a hand shape, indicating there is a hyperlink. Clicking on the thumbnail will hyperlink to the larger image. The *Note* about the restrictions on PhotoDraw content comes from Microsoft itself. While PhotoDraw content may be used for any pictures you create, it cannot be used in any picture that may become a logo or trademark. This might be a good opportunity to remind learners of copyright issues, particularly as they relate to the Internet. Just because you can take an image or document from the Web does not mean you can use it without permission.

Adding Web Buttons and Banners begins the next step in the process, adding content to the page. Help learners understand what a hyperlink is and how it works. Ask them how they know, when they are on the Internet, which word or picture they can click on when visiting a Web site. When the pointer changes to a hand it indicates they are resting over a hyperlink. Help them also understand that each Web site on the Internet has a URL that functions as its address.

Just as with Web backgrounds, Web buttons can be created by using templates or from scratch. Creating a button by using a template also follows the same steps as using templates for other functions. However, when the learners are finished creating their Web button they will see it as a separate object. This may be a good time to review the concept of objects with your learners. Everything in a PhotoDraw picture is an object, and these can be individually moved and changed as needed.

Step-By-Step 3.3 directs learners though the steps for creating a button with a template and then applying a 3-D effect. Sometimes applying 3-D effects can be difficult for learners. This effect can be applied to either the text on the button or the button itself. It is important that the entire button first be selected, not just the text.This takes a little bit of dexterity to be sure that the button is the selected object. This may be a good time to discuss the Microsoft Undo (and Redo) buttons and how helpful they can be.

To create a button from scratch, there is an almost endless array of possibilities. The basic process is to choose a shape and then apply a style and various effects. First, begin by determining the shape to be used, then add a style if desired, and finally tack on the special effects that make the button look so dazzling. Step-By-Step 3.4 is an activity that helps learners create a button from scratch.

Of course the buttons don't just sit on the page; they have two important functions: They serve as hyperlinks and they also dress up a page by adding a rollover effect or animated GIF. A rollover effect changes the appearance of a button when you move the mouse over it (called hovering) or when you click on it. An animated GIF makes the button dance on the screen without moving the mouse over it. These are both very sophisticated button effects, but PhotoDraw makes them easy to create. Remember, when using a button as a hyperlink, you can either go to another location on the Web or to a file on your computer.

Step-By-Step 3.5 applies hyperlinks, rollovers, and animated GIFs to buttons. Allow learners time to explore the different types of animated GIFs. Remind them that you don't want a bouncing button to overwhelm the content of the page!

A banner is a horizontal message that stretches across a page. Banners are used to attract the attention of Web visitors. Like a Web button, a banner can be created using either a template or from scratch and it can also have a hyperlink associated with it. The two types of banners are advertising banners, used to display information, and site banners that are used to hyperlink to another Web page. As with all templates, you can change the graphic or the text as necessary. However, when changing a graphic on a banner it may be difficult to see because the graphic is transparent. Remind your learners that since a banner is another object it can be moved as needed. Step-By-Step 3.6 creates an advertising banner, changes its background image, and places it on the Web page.

The *Hot Tip* on page 43 provides a shortcut for previewing a picture in a browser. PhotoDraw has several keystroke shortcuts, which are standard in all Microsoft Office programs. Try to identify which commands you use the most and determine whether there is a keystroke shortcut. You can save considerable time by using them. The *Hot Tip* regarding the picture list reveals that the small arrow next to a picture in the list will show all of the objects that make up that picture. This can be very useful when you need to dissect a picture because you forgot how it was constructed! The *Hot Tip* on the left arrow in the workpane will allow the learner to see all of the choices in the workpane instead of having to scroll through them. This can be useful, especially when there are numerous choices. When hyperlinking to a file on your computer, as the *Note* on page 50 points out, you are not using the Hypertext Markup Protocol (HTTP) to reach that file. The HTTP protocol is only used on the Internet. Therefore, the prefix is not HTTP:// but rather file://.

Preview and Save rounds out the steps in creating a Web page with PhotoDraw. Sometimes it is difficult to visualize how Web pages containing special effects will appear when viewed over the Internet. PhotoDraw allows you to start your browser program and actually see what your page will look like in a Web browser. Remind the learners to be patient when using Preview; it may take several seconds for PhotoDraw to render the picture into HTML code and launch the browser. Saving the picture as HTML can be done by using the Save For Use In wizard, which was introduced in the previous chapter. Don't spend too much time discussing different file types; these will be covered in more detail later. The Step-By-Step activity 3.7 previews the page in a browser and then saves it as HTML code with the Save For Use In wizard. The *Note* on the optimum screen resolution is strictly a "lowest common denominator" figure. If you're confident that most site visitors will browse your page at a higher screen resolution, you should choose one of the higher resolution sizes, such as 750 × 550 pixels.

Close

Have learners complete the end-of-lesson *Vocabulary Review* and *Review Questions. Vocabulary Review* requires learners to provide written definitions for key terms from the lesson. The *Review Questions* test learners' understanding of lesson concepts, requiring them to think critically about ideas discussed in class.

Project 3-1 directs learners to create a background using a template and change the resolution to 600 × 800.

Project 3-2 involves retrieving a file and creating a banner and two buttons using templates. A rollover, Animated Gif effect, and hyperlinks are then added to the buttons.

Project 3-3 asks the learner to create a Web page for an ice cream store. You may want to encourage learners to sketch their design on paper before starting the work. Having other learners review the design and make comments can be very helpful at this step. It's always easier to change something on paper than it is after the page is finished. If your computers have direct connection to the Internet, learners will be asked to create another button that links to an appropriate Web site. You may want to give them a list of sites from which to choose, or spend time helping them use a search engine.

Critical Thinking has learners create a Web page for their own personal use or for a small company. This can easily become a group project as well. When all of the pages are completed, the entire group can review them and make both positive and negative criticisms.

Assess

Assign the Lesson 3 Test located on the *Electronic Instructor* CD-ROM.

Vocabulary

Hypertext Markup Language (*HTML*)—The language that a Web browser program understands and translates into words and images to be viewed on a computer screen

picture elements (*pixels*)—Dots on a computer screen, measured horizontally and vertically, that make up an image or text

transparent—A function that makes a picture look faded because it allows a background color to bleed through it

PhotoDraw content—PhotoDraw pictures, included with the program, that anyone can use

hyperlink—A connection that allows a web surfer to jump quickly from one Web page to another with a click of the mouse

Uniform Resource Locator (*URL*)—The location or address of a Web page on the Internet

rollover—An effect that changes the appearance of a Web button when you move the mouse over it or when you click on it

animated GIF—An effect that makes a Web button move on the screen without moving the mouse pointer over it

LESSON 4 *Using Draw*

Teaching Materials

- Lesson 4 of the learner textbook
- Online access to PhotoDraw Home Page
- Lesson 4 Test from *Electronic Instructor* CD-ROM

Prepare

- Introduce the new vocabulary for this lesson, as presented in the *Vocabulary* list on the first page of the lesson.
- Remind learners that the purpose of the sidebar items, embedded in the text of the lesson, is to provide important background information. Boxed sidebar items occur under these three headings throughout the book: *Note*, *Internet*, and *Hot Tip*.
- The class can access South-Western Educational Publishing's PhotoDraw Web site for additional information and links to other related Web sites.

Teach

This chapter introduces one of PhotoDraw's very powerful tools, Draw. Along with its sibling Paint, it provides the PhotoDraw user with a wealth of resources and flexibility. Predictably, Microsoft has added numerous enhancements to both tools that not only make them very powerful but easy to use as well.

Drawing Lines and Curves begins by making a distinction between Draw and Paint. It is very important that learners begin to see that these two tools are not the same and do not perform the same functions. The analogy between an artist and an architect should be emphasized. Although we sometimes use the verbs draw and paint synonymously, they can have very different meanings in a given context. Quite simply, you draw for precision and you paint for expression. This is the fundamental difference between PhotoDraw's Draw and Paint tools. With Paint tools you can create expressive freehand lines and shapes. The Draw tools, on the other hand, let you create and edit very precise lines and shapes.

The first Draw tool is the most basic: Line. Although there are different ways of using this tool, the simplest way to start is to click on the Line icon on the Standard toolbar. In the workpane there is a gallery of line shapes to choose from, as well as options for selecting the width of the line and its color. Then, click the starting point of the line, drag to the ending point, and release the mouse button. This will draw a straight line. Allow learners to experiment freely with drawing lines until they become comfortable with the process. The ruler bars at the top and side of the workspace are helpful when drawing lines. Assist learners in drawing two lines that are the same length by using the ruler bars. Again, the ruler bars reinforce Draw as a tool of precision. Step-By-Step 4.1 creates a letterhead with three parallel lines. The greatest challenge is making the lines the same length and the ruler bars are invaluable here.

Line is not the only Draw tool available. PhotoDraw has three different types of curves that can be drawn: Curve, Freeform, and Scribble. The Curve tool will draw a curved line. Freeform is used to draw an object with both curved and straight segments. Scribble will create an object that looks like it was drawn freehand with a pen. It is very important that learners see the difference between these tools. A good activity is to give them a list of things to draw and ask them to use each of the three tools and then decide which tool is the best for a specific job. Learners should see that all three tools are essential, but generally one tool is better than the others in a given situation. Be sure that learners understand that the word curve is used to refer to the category of these three tools as well as the name of one of the tools. It can be confusing!

To draw a curve, click on the down arrow next to the Curve icon to open up the submenu and click on the Curve icon. The mouse pointer will turn into a cross shape. Click on the background where you want the curve to start. Move the mouse pointer (you do not need to drag it) to the middle of the curve and click again where you want the curve to bend. Finally, move the mouse to the point where you want the curve to end and double-click. Allow learners time to experiment with drawing curves. The most common mistake is single-clicking instead of double-clicking when you have completed the curve.

The Scribble tool is used to create an object that looks like it was drawn freehand. Click on the Scribble icon. Drag the mouse pointer in the shape that you want. PhotoDraw will draw a thin black outline of your shape as you draw. When you release the mouse button, that outline will become the size and color you selected on the workpane. Scribble is the simplest of the three tools to use.

To draw a freeform figure, click on the Freeform icon. Drag the mouse pointer in the shape that you want. PhotoDraw will again draw a thin black outline of your shape as you draw. However, unlike Scribble, when you release the mouse button the final figure will not be formed. Instead, you can continue to draw a straight line with Freeform, by moving (not dragging) the mouse pointer in the direction of the line. To complete a figure in Freeform you must double click the mouse. Freeform is the most difficult of the three tools but it has the most power.

One aspect of these tools that is sometimes frustrating is drawing multiple shapes in succession. After each figure is drawn, it is necessary to click again on the appropriate icon to select it and draw the next figure.

No discussion about these tools would be complete without a reminder of how to correct mistakes. The Undo button is vital. Learners should become very familiar with it (and its sibling, Redo) because it will prevent considerable stress. Also, selecting an object and pressing **Delete** will remove a mistake.

Step-By-Step 4.2 adds a freehand *S* to the letterhead created in the previous activity as well as a text object.

The *Internet* tip about the firing of employees because of inappropriate e-mail should encourage learners to question the privacy of e-mail. Many are shocked to learn that privacy laws do not protect e-mail messages as they do a letter sent through the Postal Service. Even the US Supreme Court has ruled that employers have the right to monitor an employee's e-mail. An old rule of thumb is, only put into an e-mail message what you would want posted on a bulletin board for anyone to read! The *Note* on the differences and similarities between Paint and Draw is important. Learners may often be confused about which tool to use at a given time. The basic rule of thumb is: Draw when you want to be exact and Paint when you want to be expressive. The analogy regarding the architect and the artist at the beginning of the chapter should be helpful. The *Hot Tip* about the icon on the Standard toolbar should be stressed to learners to avoid confusion. Microsoft's adaptive technology, hailed by some and scorned by others, attempts to adjust the work environment to the user. With all Office 2000 products, menu choices that are used frequently are automatically moved up to the top of the menu list, while those not used as much fall to the bottom. Many educators have complained that this adaptive technology is a hindrance to novice users who like to see the same thing in the same place. The easiest solution for beginners is to click on the down arrow next to whichever icon is displayed, opening up a menu with all three of the Curve choices. The *Note* about when to use Curve, Scribble, or Freehand helps learners understand the differences between the tools and when they should be used. Scribble is strictly a loose format, like picking up a pen to doodle. Curve draws structured curved lines. Freehand falls somewhere in between the two.

Drawing Shapes rounds out the discussion on Draw tools. A shape is a ready-made object and includes lines, basic shapes like squares or circles, flowchart elements, buttons, and other design shapes. There are two types of shapes available in PhotoDraw. Microsoft Office AutoShapes are found in all of the Microsoft Office programs (Word, Excel, etc.). They generally have one or more diamond-shaped selection handles that let you change both the appearance of the shape as well as its size.

One way to change the appearance of a shape is to use edit points. An edit point is a place on the shape where two lines meet or, in the case of a curve, the highest point of the curve, or the end of the curve. You may want to draw several shapes and have learners identify the edit points. PhotoDraw allows you to add or remove edit points. An instructive activity involves selecting a shape and then adding and removing several of its edit points. Learners can quickly see how these points make up the shape and how the shape can be altered.

The other type of shape available is called a PhotoDraw Shape and includes filled buttons, designer shapes, and simple shape outlines. Although you can resize PhotoDraw Shapes, you cannot reshape them as you can AutoShapes because there are no edit points in PhotoDraw Shapes to manipulate.

Step-By-Step 4.3 adds two shapes to the letterhead.

Unanticipated volume has been the bane of many an Internet site. Britannica experienced one of the most recently publicized problems, as the *Internet* tip on page 63 reveals. When it posted the entire contents of its encyclopedia set on the Web, it anticipated up to 1 million hits per day. However, the interest of the Internet public was ten times that amount on just the first day, clogging the systems and skyrocketing response times. Much to its credit, Britannica quickly responded by adding an astonishing 72 additional servers. Deleting an edit point, as shown in the *Hot Tip* on page 64, simply involves holding the **Ctrl** key and clicking on that point. Be aware, however, that deleting a point can do strange things to a shape! The *Note* on using Draw to create an oblong shape shows just how versatile this tool can be. A shape that you create can be added to the shapes gallery, as pointed out in the *Hot Tip*. Adding it is a simple step and makes it available for future use. The recent action by states like North Carolina and Vermont, to regulate Internet on-line auctions, is the topic of the *Internet* tip on page 67. This is not the result of new legislation passed by these states. Rather, it is an effort to enforce existing laws that require anyone who conducts a public auction to have a license. Although Internet auctions were unknown to the framers of these laws, enforcing the legislation has again raised the issue of how much should old laws, never intended to address the Internet age, be applied to the Web? You may want your learners to do some additional research in this area and identify laws, passed before the Internet existed, that have been offered up as a means of regulating or policing Web activity. Of course, the issue of taxation of Internet commerce is at the forefront of this debate.

Close

Have learners complete the end-of-lesson *Vocabulary Review* and *Review Questions. Vocabulary Review* requires learners to provide written definitions for key terms from the lesson. The *Review Questions* test learners' understanding of lesson concepts, requiring them to think critically about ideas discussed in class.

Project 4-1 directs learners to create a business card using text objects, lines, and shapes.

Project 4-2 involves retrieving a file and adding a shape. It also involves using the Draw tools of Line, Curve, Freeform, and Scribble to write your name. Be aware, this can be a frustrating activity! Learners will quickly see that it's not as easy as it seems. Be sure to stress that they need to use different tools to create different letters and numbers. You may even want to ask them to keep track of which tool is best for creating a particular letter or number.

Project 4-3 asks the learner to create a diskette label using shapes and text objects.

Critical Thinking has learners reproduce an audio CD insert using PhotoDraw's Draw tools. Be sure that they are not too ambitious at first. The CD they should attempt to copy should not be too involved but should still offer a challenge. You may even want to have some of your own CD's for learners to view as prospective samples.

Assess

Assign the Lesson 4 Test located on the *Electronic Instructor* CD-ROM.

Vocabulary

Freeform—A Draw tool used to form an object with both curved and straight segments

Scribble—A Draw tool that will create an object that looks like it was drawn freehand with a pen

deselected—An icon button that is no longer selected

shape—A ready-made object, including lines, basic shapes like squares or circles, flowchart elements, buttons, and other design shapes

edit point—A place on the shape where two lines meet, the highest point of a curve, or the end of a curve

LESSON 5 *Using Paint*

Teaching Materials

- Lesson 5 of the learner textbook
- Online access to PhotoDraw Home Page
- Lesson 5 Test from *Electronic Instructor* CD-ROM

Prepare

- Introduce the new vocabulary for this lesson, as presented in the *Vocabulary* list on the first page of the lesson.
- Remind learners that the purpose of the sidebar items, embedded in the text of the lesson, is to provide important background information. Boxed sidebar items occur under these three headings throughout the book: *Note*, *Internet*, and *Hot Tip*.
- The class can access South-Western Educational Publishing's PhotoDraw Web site for additional information and links to other related Web sites.

Teach

This lesson introduces the second of PhotoDraw's very powerful tools, Paint. Along with its sibling Draw, it provides the PhotoDraw user with a wealth of power and flexibility. As could be expected, Microsoft has added numerous enhancements to both tools that make them not only easy to use but very powerful as well.

Working With Paint Tools begins by making a distinction between Draw and Paint. It is very important that learners understand that these two tools are not the same and do not perform the same functions. The comparison between an artist and an architect should be emphasized. Although we sometimes use the verbs draw and paint synonymously, they do have specific differences. Quite simply, you draw for precision and you paint for expression. This is also the difference between PhotoDraw's Draw and Paint tools. Paint tools enable you to create expressive freehand lines and shapes while the Draw tools let you create and edit very precise lines and shapes.

PhotoDraw divides its Paint tools into two categories: paintbrushes and other painting tools. You may ask your learners what an artist uses to create a picture. Usually we think of paintbrushes as the tool of choice but many artists use other tools, such as chalk, charcoal, or pencil, to create their works. Help learners to see that the great variety of artists tools are similar to those found in Photo Draw.

This variety of painting tools illustrates just how powerful Paint can be. Some of these tools might never be used by most artists but they can be used in PhotoDraw to create some stunning effects. Allow learners to experiment with the different tools so they can begin to gain a feel for their similarities and differences. However, be sure they keep the size of the tool the same when comparing. A thick pencil line is much different than a thin highlighter line.

The Paint floating toolbar is also displayed along with the workpane. A floating toolbar can be moved anywhere on the screen by clicking on its blue title bar and dragging it to a new location. Show learners how to move the floating toolbar so it is close to the object which they are working. This minimizes mouse movements and really speeds up the work.

Clip art is introduced here. Learners will probably be familiar with it from other Microsoft Office programs. Although it sometimes has a cartoon effect, it can still be used effectively in many situations. PhotoDraw has its own additions to clip art, found on the accompanying CD-ROM.

No discussion about these tools would be complete without a reminder of how to correct mistakes. The Undo button is vital. Learners should become very familiar with it (and its sibling, Redo) because it will save considerable stress. Also, selecting the object and pressing Delete will remove a mistake.

Step-By-Step 5.1 inserts a clip art and then uses Paint to add to the picture.

The *Note* about locating the Paint floating toolbar close to the object you are working on may seem obvious, but it's amazing how many learners position the toolbar nowhere near their worksites and then end up reaching farther for it than they would the Standard toolbar!

Creating Objects with Artistic Brushes introduces learners to the second type of Paint tool called Artistic Brushes. Artistic Brushes can create a picture that resembles what an artist would create using brushes or similar tools. To create a picture using one of Paint's Artistic Brushes, click on **Draw Paint** and then on **Artistic Brushes.** This will display the gallery of over 75 different brush types, each intended to imitate what an artist would create by using that tool on a canvas. Some of the brush types are what we would expect an artist to use (such as *Dry Brush–Smooth* and *Oil–Heavy Wide*) while others are very unusual (like *Stamp–French Fry, Newsprint* and *Fax–Stairstep*). This variety gives you a great deal of control over how the final picture will look.

Step-By-Step 5.2 uses an artistic brush to enhance a picture.

The *Hot Tip* about the *Undo Last* button on the floating toolbar can be very helpful. When you paint several lines one after another, PhotoDraw considers all of the lines to be one object. If you were to try to select and delete one line out of several, you would not be able to do so. The *Undo Last* button will allow you to selectively delete lines. The *Note* on expanding the artistic brushes gallery is especially helpful when trying to choose between many different options that may look similar.

Modify Objects with Brushes completes the discussion on Paint tools. Because everything in PhotoDraw is an object, including pictures created with Artistic Brushes, any object can easily be modified with other artistic brushes. To modify the picture made with an artistic brush with another artistic brush style, click on that image in the workspace to select it. Then, click on a new type of artistic brush style. The image will then be changed to that style. Not only can an artistic brush image be modified by another artistic brush style, it can also be changed with an entirely different brush type. Clicking on the down arrow in the workpane next to *Artistic Brushes* will display the menu of other brush types available. These include Plain, Theme Brushes, and Photo Brushes. The look of Theme Brushes may be familiar because PhotoDraw has several themes that it runs consistently through many different templates. Parts of those themes are found here in Theme Brushes. A photo brush is composed of photographic images that can be manipulated (stretched, curved, etc.) as needed. These add a dazzling effect to a picture.

Similar to Photo Brushes are Photo Stamps. Unlike a photo brush, that creates a continuous unbroken line of an image, Photo Stamps are individual photographic images that appear in random sizes and positions as you paint with them. Click on **Draw Paint** and then on **Photo Stamps** to open the workpane.

As stated in the *Internet* tip on page 78, the new law entitled the Children's Online Privacy Protection Act was the direct result of unscrupulous Web sites gaining personal information on children and then using it without their knowledge or consent. This law attempts to limit the gathering of that type of information from Children under 13. However, the law does not apply to adults and many Web sites are gathering information on their visitors without informing them. The *Internet* tip on how much Web surfers spend on the Internet is enlightening. The more experience a surfer has, the more they tend to buy. You may ask your learners to list reasons why first-time users are reluctant to buy over the Internet (giving out credit card information, unsure of return policies, etc.). You may also want to visit several Web sites and see how these concerns are addressed. The growth of e-commerce on the Internet is the topic of the *Internet* tip on page 81. Sales have skyrocketed, with close to $12 billion dollars sold over the Internet during the Christmas 1999 season. Traditional "brick and mortar" stores are scrambling to create their own Web presence to prevent a dramatic drop in sales as consumers adjust to this new way of shopping. The big winners, of course, are the package delivery companies! The random size and shape of photo stamps can be changed to a uniform position and spacing, as pointed out in the *Hot Tip* on page 82.

Close

Have learners complete the end-of-lesson *Vocabulary Review* and *Review Questions. Vocabulary Review* requires learners to provide written definitions for key terms from the lesson. The *Review Questions* test learners' understanding of lesson concepts, requiring them to think critically about ideas discussed in class.

Project 5-1 directs learners to import a clip art image and then use one of the Paint tools to create a flyer.

Project 5-2 involves retrieving a file and adding an artistic brush shape. Then, a text object is placed over the shape.

Project 5-3 asks the learner to create a letterhead using text objects, photo brushes, and photo stamps. As a variation, you may ask your learners to select at random another brush or stamp that they prefer.

Critical Thinking has learners duplicate an artist's sketch using PhotoDraw's Paint tools. Be sure that they are not too ambitious initially. The sketch they choose to reproduce should not be too involved but should still pose a challenge. You may even want to have some of your own sketches for learners to view as prospective samples.

Assess

Assign the Lesson 5 Test located on the *Electronic Instructor* CD-ROM.

Vocabulary

floating toolbar—A toolbar that can be moved anywhere on the screen by clicking on its blue title bar and dragging it to a new location

clip art—Graphic images that are already drawn and can be incorporated into pictures

Artistic Brushes—Special PhotoDraw Paint brushes that can create a picture that resembles what an artist would create using brushes or similar tools

Theme Brushes—A type of PhotoDraw Paint brush that can create a picture of colorful lines and symbols

Photo Brushes—Unique PhotoDraw Paint brushes that can create a picture made up of a continuous, unbroken line of a photographic image

Photo Stamps—Small, individual photos that can be repeated to form a line

LESSON 6 *Opening, Inserting, and Saving Images*

Teaching Materials

- Lesson 6 of the learner textbook
- Online access to PhotoDraw Home Page
- Lesson 6 Test from *Electronic Instructor* CD-ROM

Prepare

- Introduce the new vocabulary for this lesson, as presented in the *Vocabulary* list on the first page of the lesson.
- Remind learners that the purpose of the sidebar items, embedded in the text of the lesson, is to provide important background information. Boxed sidebar items occur under these three headings throughout the book: *Note*, *Internet*, and *Hot Tip*.
- The class can access South-Western Educational Publishing's PhotoDraw Web site for additional information and links to other related Web sites.

Teach

This lesson acquaints the learner with the tools to open, insert, and save different types of images. Although learners have been using the basics of opening and saving since the beginning, additional options which make the process much more flexible are discussed here.

Opening Files begins with a subtle but important distinction. When you are opening a file it is assumed that the file is located on your computer or on a network drive to which you have access. Later in the chapter, when the discussion turns to inserting images, the assumption is that these images are not contained in such a file but rather come from another source. Be sure that learners see this distinction now in order to avoid confusion later.

What a file contains is the first order of business, which brings us to file formats. The default file format for PhotoDraw is the MIX format. Remind learners that unless there is a compelling reason not to do so, all PhotoDraw pictures should be saved in this format. The advantage to saving a PhotoDraw picture as a MIX file is that this file format retains all of the PhotoDraw objects that you used to create the picture and you can easily reopen a MIX file and make changes to the objects. If, however, you save a PhotoDraw picture in a file format other than MIX, you lose the ability to make changes to individual objects in the picture.

PhotoDraw can save a picture in any one of 21 different file formats. The three most common formats are GIF, JPEG, and PNG. You may want to show learners an image that was saved in each of these three formats. They probably will not be able to see much difference between them at first glance. However, each format has its own set of advantages and disadvantages. The basic rule of thumb is that JPEG should be used first, GIF as the next alternative, and PNG as the final choice. However, PNG is rapidly gaining steam and will replace GIF as an alternative format. Something that has hastened the demise of GIF is the fact that this is actually a proprietary file format owned by Compuserve, and royalties are in some instances required. PNG is an open file format. You may want to have your learners do some additional research in the capabilities of PNG and see what PNG files they can locate on the Web.

Opening a file can be done by the standard *Open* from the *File* menu or using *Visual Open,* which displays a thumbnail of each file. Encourage your learners to use *Visual Open* instead of *Open;* it's much easier to find that file you're hunting for when you can quickly see its contents. This may be a good time to talk about how to create good file names. With 255 characters available for naming a file, it's unfortunate that we still have to hunt for what we want! Help learners develop a system for naming files that makes sense to them. Also, review here your requirements for naming files for assignments as well.

Step-By-Step 6.1 opens an image from the PhotoDraw CD-ROM using *Visual Open* and also opens a PNG file using standard *Open.* Be sure that students have access to this CD-ROM or show them where these files are stored on the hard drive

The sale of Internet names is the topic of the *Internet* tip on page 90. Prices have skyrocketed as individuals who registered a popular name have been able to make a tidy profit by selling it to someone else. Some additional recent sales include AltaVista.com ($3.25 million), Wine.com ($3 million), Autos.com ($2.2 million), WallStreet.com ($1.03 million), and eFlowers.com ($1 million).

Inserting Images introduces learners to the process of inserting an image from a digital camera, a graphic image file, or the Internet into a PhotoDraw project. If you have a digital camera, now is a great time to introduce it to users. The price and performance of digital cameras have made them quite affordable. Several very good models are available for under $100 and include LCD displays, built-in flashes, and even timers. Models without these features cost even less. The critical factor with a digital camera is the resolution. A camera that takes 640 × 480 is the standard; anything above that is called a megapixel and will result in higher resolution. However, if these pictures are to be used just on Web pages or as PhotoDraw images, the higher resolution becomes less important. That's because most computer monitors are not set to see those higher resolutions.

Inserting a graphics file involves retrieving an image from PhotoDraw content. This was already covered in a previous chapter so students will just need to refresh themselves with the process again.

Inserting an image from a Web page is more involved. You may want to review multitasking with the students so they feel comfortable leaving (but not exiting) PhotoDraw to launch their Web browser to find the image they want. (Although you can surf via the small windows that PhotoDraw uses for *Open from Web Page,* they are not intended for that.) PhotoDraw will display the message *Double click to open* on any image that it can retrieve.

The Step-By-Step 6.2 opens a graphic image and also retrieves an image from the Web.

The *Hot Tip* shows how to change the setup of a digital camera. Just click on **Tools,** then on **Options,** and finally click on the **Scanner/Camera** tab. The *Note* concerning the *Easy Download* button indicates that the camera can support some of PhotoDraw's expanded functions. The *Internet* tip about what Web surfers buy on the Internet is enlightening. Computer hardware accounts for over $200 million in sales. What is especially interesting are those items at the bottom of the top ten list. Food/groceries accounted for $37 million in sales, and 39% of those purchases were gifts. There is a definite trend towards using the Internet to purchase everyday consumables. The *Note* about scanning images suggests an alternative means for acquiring digital images. Although the popularity of scanning has decreased in direct proportion to the increased popularity of digital cameras, scanned pictures are still used today. The drawback is that resolution is lost in the scanning process and the final image is not as clear as the original photograph. Of course, this is not a problem with digital cameras. The *Hot Tip* about opening a picture in Internet Explorer (IE) 5.0+ can be very helpful. Right-clicking on an image in IE and then selecting *Open Picture in Microsoft PhotoDraw* can save several steps when compared to doing it with PhotoDraw's *Open from Web Page.* If you have access to IE you may ask learners to try it both ways to see which they prefer.

Saving Images completes the discussion. If you want to save an image in a format other than GIF, JPEG, or PNG, in the *Save* dialog box click on the **down arrow** next to *Save as type* to select the format in which you want to save it. To save a file as either a GIF or JPEG, click on **File** and then on **Save For Use In** to start the wizard. Select **On the Web** and click on **Next.** PhotoDraw then asks how do you want to use this picture: *As a picture* (the actual size), *As a thumbnail* (96 × 96 pixels), or *As a Web page* (an HTML document). The next dialog box asks how you want your picture saved: one size of GIF and four sizes of JPEG (*Best, High Quality, Medium Quality,* and *Low Quality*). Remind learners that if this image is to be placed on a Web page, the quality of the picture and the length of time to download the picture must be considered. A picture with higher resolution will take longer to load onto someone's browser, while a picture of lower resolution will not take as long to load. You can click on the **down arrow** next to *Connection Speed* to select the speed that most viewers will be using when visiting your Web page, then use the horizontal slider bar to view the different options.

To save an image in a PNG format, start the **Save For Use In** wizard, select **In A Microsoft Word or Similar Document,** and then click on **Next.** Finally, click on **Save** to name your file.

Step-By-Step 6.3 retrieves a picture and saves it as a JPEG file.

The *Note* regarding the MIX format used by Microsoft Picture It! reveals that MIX is becoming an important format in the eyes of Microsoft. As Microsoft incorporates its proprietary file formats into multiple Microsoft products, it's usually a good sign that it's starting to push this format as a de facto standard. Look for more Microsoft products to support it in the near future If you want to save an image in a format other than GIF, JPEG or PNG, as the *Hot Tip* on page 97 points out, just click on the down arrow next to *Save as type* to select the format you want it saved in.

Close

Have learners complete the end-of-lesson *Vocabulary Review* and *Review Questions. Vocabulary Review* requires learners to provide written definitions for key terms from the lesson. The *Review Questions* test learners' understanding of lesson concepts, requiring them to think critically about ideas discussed in class.

Project 6-1 directs learners to open an image from the PhotoDraw CD-ROM using *Visual Open* and also opens a PNG file using standard *Open.* Be sure that students have access to this CD-ROM or show them where these files are stored on the hard drive.

Project 6-2 involves retrieving a file and then inserting an image from the Internet. You may want to have a list of approved sites from which learners can retrieve an image.

Project 6-3 asks the learners to retrieve a file and then save it as a PNG file.

Critical Thinking has learners use a digital camera to take a picture or retrieve an image from the Internet and then insert it into PhotoDraw and save it as a PNG file. You may want to take pictures with the digital camera yourself and allow students to download these images into their computers instead of allowing them to take pictures.

Assess

Assign the Lesson 6 Test located on the *Electronic Instructor* CD-ROM.

Vocabulary

GIF (*Graphics Interchange Format*)—A file format that can display a maximum of 256 colors of an image and is best for black-and-white line drawings, color clip art, and pictures that use large blocks of solid colors

JPEG (*Joint Photographic Experts Group*)—A file format that is used to display high-quality images containing thousands or even millions of colors and is a common format for Web images

PNG (*Portable Network Graphics*)—A new file format designed to replace GIF because images saved in PNG can display more colors than an image saved in GIF yet the file size is smaller

file extension—A period followed by three letters in a file name that indicates the type of file format it contains

Visual Open—A PhotoDraw option that displays a thumbnail of the contents of each file.

TWAIN (*Technology Without An Interesting Name*) *software drivers*—Software that allows a digital camera to communicate with PhotoDraw and other programs

LESSON 7 *Arranging Objects*

Teaching Materials

- Lesson 7 of the learner textbook
- Online access to PhotoDraw Home Page
- Lesson 7 Test from *Electronic Instructor* CD-ROM

Prepare

- Introduce the new vocabulary for this lesson, as presented in the *Vocabulary* list on the first page of the lesson.
- Remind learners that the purpose of the sidebar items, embedded in the text of the lesson, is to provide important background information. Boxed sidebar items occur under these three headings throughout the book: *Note*, *Internet*, and *Hot Tip*.
- The class can access South-Western Educational Publishing's PhotoDraw Web site for additional information and links to other related Web sites.

Teach

This lesson introduces the tools that are used to arrange objects in a picture. These tools are very valuable and will help create a picture that has a professional look and feel to it. Microsoft has added numerous enhancements to the tools that make them not only easy to use but very powerful as well.

Resizing Objects begins with a review of how to change the size of an object. The steps for resizing an object are very basic: if the object is not selected, click on it to select it and show its handles. Then just drag one of the handles to increase or decrease its size. There are actually several different ways to resize:

1. To resize the object and maintain its proportions, drag a corner size handle.
2. To distort the look of the object by stretching or squeezing it, drag a side handle.
3. To resize an object precisely, select the object, click on **Arrange** on the visual menu, and then click on **Arrange** in the drop down menu.
   a. To maintain the proportions and keep the same relative shape for the object, select the **Maintain proportions** check box. When you enter a number in either the *Height* or the *Width* box, PhotoDraw will automatically calculate a value for the other box.
   b. To resize an object without maintaining its proportions, clear the **Maintain proportions** check box and then enter a number in the **Height** and the **Width** boxes.
4. To resize an object in one direction, select the object, click on the **Crop Size** menu, and then click on **Resize.**
5. To resize an object so that it fits the workspace, select the object and then click on the **Crop Size** menu. Click on **Resize** to display the *Resize* workpane and then select **Resize Object.** Click on the button **Fit Picture to Background.**

These different ways to resize can be confusing for learners. You may want to spend time going through each variation and point out the difference in the end results. (Be sure to start with the same image each time.) Help learners see that each of these different ways to resize objects will solve a specific problem.

Step-By-Step 7.1 inserts three PhotoDraw content pictures and resizes them.

The *Internet* tip about the Internet not being for everyone is sobering. Although the media portrays everyone in the universe as having a Web site and surfing the Internet for hours on end, such is not the case. There are many individuals who reject the use of the Internet for a myriad of valid reasons. Ask your learners why they think individuals would not want to use the Internet, or have them survey others to try to determine the reasons why. To resize the object from the center outward and still maintain its proportions, as the *Note* on page 105 indicates, press CTRL and drag a corner handle. This will maintain the correct proportions. However, to distort an object by stretching or squeezing it from the center outward, press CTRL and drag a side handle. The new law called the Anticybersquatting Consumer Protection Act went into effect in late 1999, as the *Internet* tip indicates. There have been several lawsuits in the past few years against parties who registered an Internet domain name containing a celebrity's name (like www.garthbrooks.com), or who registered a domain name similar to a trade name (like www.macdonalds.com instead of www.mcdonalds.com). The new law addresses this problem. You may want to have learners investigate the exact conditions of this law, and perhaps research how to register their own Internet domain name.

Move Objects discusses rotating, flipping, and aligning objects. Be sure that learners understand the difference between the options when using them. The option *Rotate Left* will move the object 90 degrees counter-clockwise, while *Rotate Right* will move it 90 degrees clockwise. To mirror the position of the object, click on **Flip Horizontal.** To make the object appear upside down, click on **Flip Vertical.** To flip the object both horizontally and vertically, click on **Flip Both.** Objects can be aligned by their left, right, top, or bottom edges. You can select each of the objects you want to align by holding down the **Shift** key, clicking on each of the objects, selecting **Align,** and then choosing from *Align Left, Align Right, Align Top,* or *Align Bottom.* PhotoDraw will align the objects based on their edges. To align objects horizontally by their middles or vertically by their centers, select *Align Middle* or *Align Center.*

As easy as it is to talk about this, picturing it is much more difficult. The only way to really grasp these variations is to play with them! The best approach is to select or draw an image that is not symmetrical and save that image. Apply two or three of the variations to that image and view the results. Then, reopen the original image and apply two or three more variations. Do not keep modifying a modified object! Learners will need time to play and experiment here.

Step-By-Step 7.2 rotates and aligns images.

The *Note* about moving objects by entering the exact position coordinates can be very useful for pictures that require precise locations for objects. You may want to give learners some coordinates on the workspace and have them practice moving objects. Although it is not used as often as dragging, this feature is still quite valuable. The *Internet* tip about "sticky" sites is very important from an e-commerce perspective. The longer a surfer stays at a Web site, the more likely they are to buy something. Of course the same principle holds true for shopping at traditional stores. The rest of the top five "sticky" sites are Yahoo, Microsoft Network, Excite@Home, and Go Network. Just as objects can be arranged in relation to each other, they can also be arranged in relation to the background of the picture, as the *Hot Tip* on page 109 indicates. Although this is not used as often, it can be handy at times. Another way to rotate an object, as shown in the *Note* on page 109, is to select it and then grab the bar with the green circle above the selection box. You may want to illustrate this to learners by having them do it. This gives you additional control, when rotating an object, that you cannot get from the menu.

Order Objects involves placing multiple objects in a picture and overlapping them as necessary. Be sure that learners understand that when two objects overlap, one will be in the foreground and one will be in the background. However, when more than two objects overlap, one will be in the foreground, one will be in the background, and one will be in the middle. To move an object to the foreground, click on **Bring to Front.** To move the object forward by only one position, click on **Bring Forward.** An object can be moved to the background in the same way. Select the object you want to move and then on the *Arrange* menu point to **Order.** To move the object to the back position, click on **Send to Back.** To move the object forward by only one position, click on **Send Backward.**

Another way to order objects involves using the object list from the picture list. Start with a picture composed of several objects. Then, to display the object list, click on the arrow button next to the picture that contains the object you want to reorder. The object list displays the objects that make up the picture along with the order of the objects. The higher an object appears on the object list, the closer it will be to the foreground of the workspace. To change an object's order, click on the thumbnail of that object in the object list. Drag the object upward on the list to move it to the foreground or downward on the list to move it to the background.

The Step-By-Step 7.3 activity creates a text object. It then changes the order of several other objects, adds a new object, and makes it transparent.

Turning off the object list, as shown in the *Hot Tip* on page 110, simply involves clicking on the arrow button again.

Grouping and Ungrouping Objects are unique and vital tools that can be invaluable in certain situations. To create a group, select the objects you want to include by holding down **Shift** as you click on each object. Size handles will appear around each object. Click on the **Arrange** menu and then click on **Group.** A single size handle will then appear around the objects, indicating that they are now a group. Be sure to tell learners that this is a clear indication that the group has been properly formed. In addition, the object list will show them as one object. The objects can now be manipulated as a group and anything you could do with one object you can now do with the group. To dissolve the group object and turn it back into individual objects, click on the group object to select it, click on **Arrange,** and then on **Ungroup.**

Step-By-Step 7.4 groups objects for the purpose of moving them as a unit, and then ungroups them.

The *Hot Tip* about saving in MIX format is very important. Once a picture is saved in a format other than MIX (like GIF or JPEG), the ability to manipulate objects is lost. Learners should be encouraged to always save in MIX format. If they need another format, then do a *Save As* from the MIX file.

Close

Have learners complete the end-of-lesson *Vocabulary Review* and *Review Questions. Vocabulary Review* requires learners to provide written definitions for key terms from the lesson. The *Review Questions* test learners' understanding of lesson concepts, requiring them to think critically about ideas discussed in class.

Project 7-1 directs learners to import four PhotoDraw content images and then resize them. The first object is precisely resized by using the *Arrange* workpane, while the other objects are resized by dragging. When the item is dragged, the *Arrange* workpane displays the changing height and width, dimensions which are necessary for this activity.

Project 7-2 involves retrieving a file and flipping an object. Be sure that learners look closely so they can see the difference after the flip! The objects are also aligned to the top of the card.

Project 7-3 asks the learners to retrieve a file and change the order of the objects.

Critical Thinking has learners create a letterhead using objects and the tools covered in this lesson. Be sure that they are not too ambitious but not too easy, either. You may want to have one or two samples of the level of difficulty that you will require. You may also want to specify exactly which tools or series of tools (flip, rotate, order, etc.) they must use.

Assess

Assign the Lesson 7 Test located on the *Electronic Instructor* CD-ROM.

Vocabulary

aligning objects—Moving objects so they line up with other objects by their left, right, top, or bottom edges

object list—Displays objects that make up a picture as well as the order of those objects

group objects—Combine several objects in order to treat them as a single object

ungroup objects—Dissolve a group object into individual objects

LESSON 8 *Special Effects*

Teaching Materials

- Lesson 8 of the learner textbook
- Online access to PhotoDraw Home Page
- Lesson 8 Test from *Electronic Instructor* CD-ROM

Prepare

- Introduce the new vocabulary for this lesson, as presented in the *Vocabulary* list on the first page of the lesson.
- Remind learners that the purpose of the sidebar items, embedded in the text of the lesson, is to provide important background information. Boxed sidebar items occur under these three headings throughout the book: *Note*, *Internet*, and *Hot Tip*.
- The class can access South-Western Educational Publishing's PhotoDraw Web site for additional information and links to other related Web sites.

Teach

This chapter acquaints the learner with the tools to create special effects. Special effects are commonplace today, so much so that it's often hard to tell if it is a special effect or if it's real. PhotoDraw has that same level of precision. Unless you knew otherwise, you might think it was done by an artist on a canvas.

Applying Shadow, Transparency, and Fade Out are three of the most commonly used special effects in PhotoDraw. Help learners understand the similarities and differences of each feature so they will know when to use them. A shadow effect can be particularly striking when used correctly. PhotoDraw provides a wealth of options for creating and altering different types of shadows. *Shadow Position* allows you to move the shadow by dragging it to a new position. This enables you to create the time of day you want the shadow to convey, either by lengthening the shadow or by shortening it. The *Transparency* slider makes the shadow darker (a lower number) or lighter (a higher number). *Soften* makes the shadow sharp (a lower number) or blurred (a higher number). Give your learners time to play with shadows until they have a feel for this powerful tool.

Transparency has been used previously in other lessons but more of its features are introduced here. Transparency is a function that makes a picture look faded because it allows a background color to bleed through it. Transparency can also be used to create unusual special effects. One use of Transparency is to make it appear as if you can see inside an object. You may want your learners to walk through an activity that makes something see-through. It's a good opportunity for them to hone their shadow skills.

A variation on Transparency is Fade Out. Whereas Transparency makes the entire object look faded, Fade Out allows you to control the fading in several different ways. Fade Out has several different options, including a shape for the fade, where the center of the fade lies, and how much to fade in and to fade out. Although these differences are subtle, encouraging learners to start by moving sliders to their extreme ends and then working backwards usually illustrates the differences.

Step-By-Step 8.1 has learners retrieve an image and add a shadow to it. They also adjust the shadow settings.

The *Note* on how Microsoft PhotoDraw actually creates a shadow shows that it is done much as an artist would do it. You (or any of your artistic learners) may want to demonstrate on paper how this is done.

Adding and Changing Colors allows PhotoDraw learners to delve into the wonderful world of color. You may want to begin by telling learners that nothing can influence our feelings about an image more than color can. The right color can draw us into what the image is saying while the wrong color can cause us to turn and walk away. Ask them to imagine that they are having dinner at a famous restaurant. As their meal is served, they see that all the food on their plate is the same color, and they wonder if everything will taste the same. Their dining partner's meal, on the other hand, is vibrant with greens and reds. Suddenly, they want to exchange plates!

Color helps designers differentiate and emphasize objects in a picture. A color's main attribute is its hue, or the name it is known by, such as red, blue, purple, and so on. Other aspects of color include tint, which is the result of adding white to a color, and shade, which is the result of adding black to a color. Warm colors are the colors of fire: red, orange, and yellow. Used in designs, these colors appear to advance toward the viewer. Artists use warm colors in the foregrounds of paintings to make those areas appear closer to the viewer. Cool colors such as blue, green, and purple, to name a few, are the opposite of warm colors. Cool colors appear to recede from the viewer. Artists typically use cool colors in the background of their paintings to create the illusion of distance.

PhotoDraw has several different ways to add or change the color of an object. Filling an object with color means adding color to an object. To fill an object with color, select the object and then click on **Fill.** There are several choices available under the *Fill* menu. Be sure your learners understand the differences between them. To fill an object with one color, click on the menu choice **Solid Color** to display the *Fill* workpane. However, PhotoDraw allows many more colors to select from than just those displayed as color chips. Click on **Fill** and then on **Color Scheme** to display the *More Colors* dialog box. Note that there are three tabs in this dialog box: *Color Scheme, Custom Palette,* and *True Color. Color Scheme* displays a defined set of color choices, or **scheme.** The applications in the Microsoft Office family (Word, PowerPoint, FrontPage, etc.) all have their own color schemes and PhotoDraw makes them available to you here. Clicking on the *Custom Palette* tab displays a library of up to 256 color choices called a palette. PhotoDraw has three palettes from which you can choose.

Web browsers use palettes of 256 colors to display pictures. However, not all browsers use the same palette. This difference in palettes can cause unwanted colors to appear in pictures. When you create pictures for use on the Web, you can use a browser-safe palette to be sure that the most common browser colors are used. PhotoDraw provides two such palettes. The *Web-Safe* palette contains the 216 colors that are most likely to be used in Web graphics. If a picture uses a color that is not stored in the *Web-Safe* palette, then the nearest matching color in the palette is mixed into the neighboring colors so that they blend smoothly. This technique (called dithering) works well with photographs and art that contain subtle gradations of color. The *Web-Solid Colors* palette contains the same 216 colors as the *Web-Safe* palette. If a picture uses a color that is not stored in the *Web-Solid Colors* palette, then the nearest matching color is used without blending. The 216 colors in these two palettes are the same colors found in the palettes used by Microsoft Internet Explorer, Mosaic, and Netscape Navigator. Since the *Web-Solid Colors* and *Web-Safe* palettes omit the 40 colors that vary between PCs and Macs, they're generally the best choice for cross-platform Web graphics.

Colorizing an object means that you apply variations of the same color to that object, as if you had dyed it. From the *Format* menu, click on **Color** and then on **Colorize.** Click on the color chip that you want to use. If the color you want is not displayed, click on the down arrow in the *Settings* box to display a color choice menu. The selection *Color Scheme* functions as it did when you used it to fill objects with colors. *Active Palette* will allow you to choose from the current palette. The *True Color* tab will display the widest spectrum of color choices. Finally, the opposite of colorizing is applying a **negative** effect. This will remove the colors and leave the object looking like a negative from camera film.

The challenge is for learners not to become confused by the various options. They should first focus on when to use fill and when to use colorizing. Then they can spend time experimenting with the various color options.

The Step-By-Step 8.2 activity creates three text objects and colors two of them.

The *Note* about the ability to create and edit your own palettes demonstrates just how flexible PhotoDraw can be when it comes to colors. The advantage of creating your own palette is that you can develop a standard set of colors that you use repeatedly without having to search for them in different locations. The *Note* concerning the number of colors in True Color shows how extensive color capabilities have become. Although the human eye can distinguish between more than 16 million, this number is still sufficient for computer images. The *Hot Tip* on page 127 shows that if you need to leave white areas intact in the object when colorizing, move the *Amount* slider to the right. Or, to increase the selected object's intensity and leave black areas in the object intact, move the *Amount* slider to the left or enter a smaller value in the *Amount* box.

Distorting Images can sometimes be useful to attract attention or to create a special emphasis. However, be sure to stress to learners that distorting for the sake of distorting is distorted! If a distorted image repels someone, then it's certainly not drawing a viewer's attention to the image. The resolution of PhotoDraw objects can be made fuzzy or sharp by using the blur or sharpen tools. PhotoDraw also includes several predefined distort effects called Designer Effects. They are a fascinating PhotoDraw tool and should not be overlooked. There are over 200 different Designer Effects. Allow learners to go through this gallery and experiment with the effects that appeal to them. To distort only a portion of the object, you can click on *Distort by painting.*

The Step-By-Step 8.3 inserts a PhotoDraw Content picture and applies a Designer Effect and also uses Distort by painting.

The founder of the World Wide Web, as the *Internet* tip points out, was actually interested in brain associations. Tim Berners-Lee at the European Particle Physics Laboratory (known as CERN) proposed that the computers can store random associations just as the brain can. He envisioned a global hypertext space in which any network-accessible information could be referenced by a single uniform resource identifier. In late 1990, Tim published the specifications for uniform resource locators (URLs), HyperText Markup Language (HTML), and HyperText Transfer Protocol (HTTP). And the rest, as they say, is history. The *Internet* tip about America Online being the first ISP to charge a flat monthly rate actually has an interesting story behind it. The result of AOL's decision caused several major problems. AOL was totally unprepared for the demand it created. New subscriptions increased 1 million in the month in which the change was announced. Members logged on and stayed on, frustrating other learners who only got busy signals or had their sessions cut off unexpectedly. In the first four weeks following this change, AOL's members logged 102 million hours of online access, compared with only 46 million hours three months before. In early 1997, AOL settled with the Attorneys General of 36 states, pledging it would improve access, upgrade its infrastructure, and issue credits. This cost the company over $400 million alone that first year. The *Internet* tip about Microsoft's reluctance to enter the Internet market is a story in itself. For several years Microsoft insisted that the PC would continue to be the foundation on which business and personal computing would be built. As the rest of the world embraced the Internet, Microsoft suddenly found itself on the outside for the first time. That, however, quickly changed when chairman Bill Gates sent out a memo in 1995, entitled "The Internet Tidal Wave," that said Microsoft was dead wrong about the Internet. "The Internet is the most important single development to come along since the [personal computer] was introduced in 1981." The *Hot Tip* on the top of page 132 gives more detailed information about using the *Distort by Painting* toolbar. To correct a mistake, click on **Restore** on the *Distort by Painting* toolbar, and then paint over the mistake. To remove your most recent stroke, click on **Undo Last.** To start over, click on **Reset.** The *Hot Tip* on the bottom of page 132 answers the question, what do I do if I want to have two or more Designer Effects on the same image? If you click another effect in the *Designer Effects* gallery, the new effect replaces the original one. To actually have two effects, you must lock the original effect so that you can combine it with another effect. This is done by clicking on *Lock Effect.*

Close

Have learners complete the end-of-lesson *Vocabulary Review* and *Review Questions. Vocabulary Review* requires learners to provide written definitions for key terms from the lesson. The *Review Questions* test learners' understanding of lesson concepts, requiring them to think critically about ideas discussed in class.

Project 8-1 directs learners to create three text objects and change the color of two of them. Then, they are to apply a shadow effect to the remaining object. You may want them to experiment with other shadow options to see the different effects.

Project 8-2 involves retrieving a file and distorting parts of it by painting.

Project 8-3 asks the learner to insert a PhotoDraw content image and then apply a Designer Effect.

Critical Thinking has learners retrieve a PhotoDraw Content image and then create three different Designer Effects. They will then ask others for input about these effects.

Assess

Assign the Lesson 8 Test located on the *Electronic Instructor* CD-ROM.

Vocabulary

Fade Out—Allows you to control the fading of an object instead of making the entire object look faded
filling—Adding color to an object
color chips—Colored squares that can be clicked on to select a color
scheme—A defined set of color choices
palette—A library of up to 256 color choices
colorizing—Applying variations of the same color to an object
negative effect—Removes the colors and leaves the object looking like a negative from camera film

LESSON 9 *Retouching Photographs*

Teaching Materials

- Lesson 9 of the learner textbook
- Online access to PhotoDraw Home Page
- Lesson 9 Test from *Electronic Instructor* CD-ROM

Prepare

- Introduce the new vocabulary for this lesson, as presented in the *Vocabulary* list on the first page of the lesson.
- Remind learners that the purpose of the sidebar items, embedded in the text of the lesson, is to provide important background information. Boxed sidebar items occur under these three headings throughout the book: *Note*, *Internet*, and *Hot Tip*.
- The class can access South-Western Educational Publishing's PhotoDraw Web site for additional information and links to other related Web sites.

Teach

This lesson introduces the tools used to retouch photographs. You may begin to ask your learners approximately how many photographs they take every year. You will find that the popularity of photography has not diminished, particularly with the introduction of disposable and digital cameras. However, it is very difficult to take a perfect photograph. All photos that must be developed are retouched in some way, and specialty photos (like portrait photographs) are given particular consideration. This lesson focuses (no pun intended!) upon the art of retouching photographs in PhotoDraw. You may want to take time to emphasize that this is the third element of PhotoDraw's features. Remember, PhotoDraw is a graphics design program used to create graphic images for use on business cards, letterheads, flyers and other printed documents. PhotoDraw is also an Internet Web design tool that can be used to create and edit graphics for Web sites. Finally, PhotoDraw is a photographic editing program that can be used to touch-up or change a photograph. PhotoDraw enables you to design, create, and edit graphic images, Web graphics, and photographs with ease.

It's important to remind learners that the degree to which you change a photograph when retouching it depends upon what you have to work with initially. A terrible photograph can only be retouched to a point! This may be an opportunity to talk about some basic rules of photography: Always have the sun to your back when taking photos outdoors; create a focal point by using lines that point to or converge in one place; light blue does not photograph well; frame your shots in the viewfinder before you take them.

The PhotoDraw tools for retouching photographs include:

- Blur and Sharpen
- Brightness and Contrast
- Correct Tint
- Hue and Saturation
- Fix Red Eye
- Remove Dust
- Remove Scratch

Correcting Focus and Brightness starts by pointing out that with advances in photographic technology, out-of-focus or dark photographs are not as common as in the past. However, it is still not unusual to have a photograph that needs to be retouched. PhotoDraw provides special tools to correct the focus or the brightness of a photograph.

A slightly out-of-focus photograph can be sharpened easily in PhotoDraw. Sometimes it is even desirable to blur a photograph intentionally to create a special look. To sharpen a photograph, open the photograph in PhotoDraw and then click on **Touchup** and then on **Blur and Sharpen** to open the *Blur and Sharpen* workpane. Drag the slider to the right or click on the up arrow to sharpen the photograph. To blur an image, drag the slider to the left or click on the down arrow.

The brightness and contrast of a photograph can also be adjusted. Be sure that your learners understand the difference between these terms. ***Brightness*** refers to how light or dark the object appears, while ***contrast*** refers to the difference between the lightest and darkest areas of the photograph. There are two ways to adjust the brightness or contrast. To let PhotoDraw adjust the brightness and contrast for you, click on the **Automatic** button on the workpane. Generally, this should be done first before trying to adjust the settings manually. To make the object appear brighter manually, move the slider to the right in the *Brightness* setting. Move the slider to the left to make it darker. To increase the contrast, move the slider to the right in the *Contrast* setting or to the left to decrease the contrast.

Step-By-Step 9.1 retrieves a PhotoDraw Content photograph, sharpens it, and then adjusts the contrast and brightness both automatically and manually.

Some low-end photographic editing programs will only sharpen an image automatically, as the *Note* on page 137 indicates. Although these programs will sometimes hit the mark, they often cannot detect small nuances in a photograph that the human eye can see. The flexibility of PhotoDraw's automatic and manual adjustment features set this program apart from the rest. The *Note* on page 139 suggests a good idea for effective use of the automatic adjustment feature of brightness and contrast. When working with brightness and contrast, let PhotoDraw automatically adjust them and then you can manually tweak the settings if necessary. The *Hot Tip* about selectively adjusting the brightness or contrast of a particular area of a photograph once again shows how powerful PhotoDraw is. *Clicking on Correct by Painting* in the workpane will allow you to indicate where, on the photograph, brightness and contrast should be changed.

Adjusting the Color describes PhotoDraw's ability to change the colors in a photograph. The first tool adjusts the tint. If you shoot a photograph indoors without a flash, the resulting image might have an overall green or reddish tint. If you have a digital camera, you may want to take several shots with the flash turned off indoors to show how it can affect the color. Color tinting also occurs when an older photograph ages over time and loses some of its color. If you have an old, yellowed photograph, it can be used to illustrate this concept. There even are times when you might want to add a color tint to a photograph to give a special effect.

As with brightness and contrast, there are two ways in which you can adjust the tint. You can let PhotoDraw adjust the tint automatically or you can adjust the tint manually. When doing it manually, however, you must select an individual color on the photograph and then adjust the tint for that color. First, from the *Touchup* menu, click on **Correct Tint.** Then, select a color by moving the **Hue** slider to the color that you want. Then, you can do either of the following: To add more of the tint color, move the **Amount** slider to the right or enter a larger value in the *Amount* box. To remove the tint color, move the Amount slider to the left or enter a smaller value in the *Amount* box. Pay particular attention to Figure 9-10 and notice that all of the green was removed from the photograph. This can be a very powerful tool!

The second PhotoDraw tool is, in a word, complicated. Modifying the hue and saturation of a photograph is a very difficult concept to grasp. Be sure that learners understand the meaning of these two terms. The ***hue*** is the color of a color. When you use a word like red or blue, you are actually naming a hue. The strength or intensity of the color is called its ***saturation.*** Saturation is the percentage of a particular hue present in a color. A completely saturated color is said to contain 100 percent of its hue.

Modifying the hue involves an understanding of colors. The ***color spectrum*** is all the colors that the human eye can see. When modifying the hue in PhotoDraw, you shift colors along this spectrum. The end result may not be what you had intended. Notice that the *Hue* slider starts at the color red (value *0*). As the slider is moved to the right towards yellow (value *50*), the colors in the picture change. However, the colors do not become yellow. Instead, the reference point of the picture is now yellow instead of red. Depending on how much experience you and the learners have had with color and its use, you may want to spend considerable time here or just let the learners experiment.

Step-By-Step 9.2 corrects the brightness, contrast and tint of a photograph.

The *Internet* tip on page 143 about the proliferation of companies with which you can register a domain name marks a major turning point in the history of the Internet. Network Solutions, Inc., had an exclusive contract with the US Government to sell and register Internet domain names (for .com names only). However, there was significant concern regarding this exclusive agreement and the way Network Solutions did business. In 1999 the agreement was "deregulated" and new registrars were allowed to enter the market. The *Internet* tip on page 145 about the length of Internet domain names will result in major changes on the Web. Prior to late 1999, a domain name was limited to 22 characters. However, several registrars competing with Network Solutions, Inc. (see previous *Internet* tip) began offering the ability to register longer names. Such names as *thebiggestpetstoreontheweb.com, largestshoppingmallintheworld.com* and *isthereadoctor inthehouse.com* have already been registered. The astonishing growth of the Internet, as illustrated in the second *Internet* tip on page 145, continues to stagger the imagination! From 1998 to 1999, the increase of US-based users climbed 23% to a total of 119 million. No wonder the Web is sometimes so slow! Floating toolbars are very useful, but they are slightly different from normal toolbars, as the *Hot Tip* on page 143 indicates. The *Undo Last* command on the floating toolbars removes the last action you performed, much like the *Redo* button on the standard toolbar. The *Reset* returns the image to its original condition before any changes were made with the floating toolbar.

Removing problems completes the discussion on photographic retouching. ***Red eye*** is a common occurrence in photographs taken with a flash attachment. Red eye occurs when the light from the flash reflects from the subject's retina back to the camera. If the flash is close to the camera lens, as it is in many small cameras, there's a good chance of red eye. If you have a digital camera with a flash attachment, you may take some shots of learners to illustrate red eye. You may also talk about how modern cameras try to prevent the problem. Some cameras have a small preflash that contracts the subject's pupil so that there is less area to reflect the real flash. To remove red eye, click on **Touchup** and then on **Fix Red Eye** to open the workpane and the *Red Eye* floating toolbar. The cursor turns into a small circle. Click the red portion of the eyes, then click on **Fix** on the *Red Eye* toolbar, and then click on **Finish.** The *Correction amount* slider indicates how large an area of red eye needs to be corrected. To create a larger area, move the slider to the right. Show students that they must first correct red eye and then they can change the correction amount.

Dust on a camera lens will produce a photograph that has speckles called dust spots. PhotoDraw can easily correct dust spots or other small imperfections in a photograph. It does this by blending together adjacent colors to smooth out any abrupt changes. To remove spots, click on **Touchup** and then on **Remove Dust** to open the workpane and the *Dust and Spots* floating toolbar. The cursor turns into a small circle. Click on the spots to be removed and then click on **Finish** on the toolbar.

The final tool, Remove Scratch, actually has several uses. Scratches appear on photographs when a reprint is made from a negative that has become scratched from handling it. PhotoDraw can erase the scratch by blending in colors from adjacent areas of the photograph. However, since digital cameras do not create negatives, this PhotoDraw touchup technique is more often used today to remove an unwanted, straight line image from a photograph. Click on **Touchup** and then on **Remove Scratch** to open the workpane and the *Scratch* floating toolbar. The *Scratch Width* slider allows you to set the width of the area that you want to remove. Start with a narrower width first. Click on the beginning of the line of objects that you want to remove and then click on its end. Click on **Finish** on the floating toolbar when completed.

Step-By-Step 9.3 corrects the brightness and contrast and then removes spots on a photograph.

Red eye does not occur in animals, as the *Note* reveals. In humans, light reflected from the retina produces a red eye affect. In animals, for some reason, it appears green. As the *Hot Tip* reveals, another difference in the floating toolbar is the *Finish* button. Once you click on *Finish* on the floating toolbar you cannot undo any of your changes.

Close

Have learners complete the end-of-lesson *Vocabulary Review* and *Review Questions. Vocabulary Review* requires learners to provide written definitions for key terms from the lesson. The *Review Questions* test learners' understanding of lesson concepts, requiring them to think critically about ideas discussed in class.

Project 9-1 directs learners to retrieve a file and adjust the brightness, contrast, and sharpness of the photograph.

Project 9-2 involves retrieving a file and correcting the tint. When asked to click on an area of the object that should be white or light gray, direct learners to click on the edge of one of the white bags containing flowers.

Project 9-3 asks the learner to retrieve a file and correct the red eye.

Critical Thinking has learners take pictures with a digital camera and correct them. As an option, you might want them to take pictures with a regular camera and have the pictures developed and then stored on a photographic CD-ROM. Don't select the option of having the photographs stored on the Internet and then downloaded. Photographs developed and then stored for download are only in GIF format; those on a CD-ROM are in JPEG format. These pictures will then be touched up using the various PhotoDraw tools:

- Blur and Sharpen
- Brightness and Contrast
- Correct Tint
- Hue and Saturation
- Fix Red Eye
- Remove Dust
- Remove Scratch

Assess

Assign the Lesson 9 Test located on the *Electronic Instructor* CD-ROM.

Vocabulary

brightness—How light or dark an object appears

contrast—The difference between the lightest and darkest areas of a photograph

hue—The color of a color

saturation—The percentage of a particular hue present in a color

color spectrum—All the colors that the human eye can see

red eye—Light from a flash attachment reflecting from the subject's retina, making it look red in a photograph

LESSON 10 *Editing Photographs*

Teaching Materials

- Lesson 10 of the learner textbook
- Online access to PhotoDraw Home Page
- Lesson 10 Test from *Electronic Instructor* CD-ROM

Prepare

- Introduce the new vocabulary for this lesson, as presented in the *Vocabulary* list on the first page of the lesson.
- Remind learners that the purpose of the sidebar items, embedded in the text of the lesson, is to provide important background information. Boxed sidebar items occur under these three headings throughout the book: *Note*, *Internet*, and *Hot Tip.*
- The class can access South-Western Educational Publishing's PhotoDraw Web site for additional information and links to other related Web sites.

Teach

You will recall from the previous lesson that retouching a photograph means to make touch-up improvements to it. These include sharpening and blurring, adjusting the brightness and contrast, removing red eye, eliminating dust spots, and removing scratches. With this lesson we introduce the companion to retouching a photograph, which is editing a photograph. Editing a photograph means to make radical changes to it, such as erasing, cropping, and cloning various elements of a photograph. Be sure that learners understand the difference between retouching and editing.

Cropping a photograph means to cut out parts of the image. PhotoDraw provides tools to make three different types of crops on a photograph. The first is to simply erase an element from a photograph. There are 56 different shapes available from the gallery that enable you to approximate the shape of the image that you want to erase. Learners may have to search to find the image that best matches the shape they wish to erase. Many of the shapes are specialty shapes like stars and hearts. The disadvantage in erasing an element is that it leaves a hole in the photograph, as Figure 10-3 illustrates. Generally, erasing would be used when you wanted one part of the photograph (such as the upper one-third) removed but the rest of it to remain untouched.

A second option for cropping involves determining which part of the photograph you want to keep and then erasing everything else. To crop a photograph, open it in PhotoDraw and then click on **Crop Size** and then on **Crop by Shape** to open the *Crop* workpane and toolbar. As before, click on one of the shapes resembling the image that you want to crop. The photograph's color will fade and the mouse pointer will change to a crosshair as you move it over the image. Click on the area that you want to cut out and when the shape you have chosen appears on the workspace, drag it over the area to be removed, using its size and rotate handles to locate it, if necessary.

The third option is to cut out a portion of the photograph without leaving a hole in it. PhotoDraw can make a copy of the element that is cut out and place it in one of several different locations for you to use. To cut out and copy a portion of a photograph, open the photograph in PhotoDraw and then click on **Crop Size** and then on **Cut Out** to open the *Cut Out* workpane and toolbar. Click on one of the shapes resembling the image that you want to cut out and copy. The entire photograph will appear as a faded color. Move the mouse pointer to the workspace and it changes to a crosshair. Click on the area of the photograph that you want to cut out and then drag the shape you have chosen over that area.

There are now three different options for placing the cutout. If you want it to be placed in a new picture by itself, check the box in the toolbar labeled *Put in new picture.* Click on **Finish** in the toolbar, and

PhotoDraw will create a new picture that contains only this cutout. If you want the cutout to be placed in the original photograph as a duplicate, uncheck the box *Put in new picture* and then click on **Finish.** A copy of the cutout will be placed directly over the original. You can drag this copy to a new location in the original photograph. The final option is to place the cutout in the Windows clipboard. If your learners are not comfortable with the clipboard, help them become familiar with it by cutting and pasting text and graphic elements into programs like Word, Excel, PhotoDraw, etc.

It would be advisable to have your learners become familiar with the three different types of cropping by having them perform all three operations on the same photograph. Select a photograph and have them erase an element. Don't save that picture, but close it and re-open the original. Then, have them crop it. Finally, do the same by cutting out a portion and saving the cutout in three different places. Emphasize that different tools are used for different purposes when editing a photograph.

Step-By-Step 10.1 has learners insert a PhotoDraw Content image and crop an area from the photograph.

The *Note* indicates that after dragging the shape, you can then resize or reposition the shape by using the resize handles or rotate handles. This is helpful because resizing or repositioning is often needed after dragging the shape. The *Internet* tip about the first e-mail message sent in 1972 indicates how common e-mail has become as a method of communication. It is estimated that in 1999 over 6.9 billion e-mail messages were sent. E-mail has become the standard mode of communication in business, often surpassing fax and telephone as the quickest way to reach someone. The *Note* about removing a crop reveals an option in the shape gallery. If you want to remove a crop, click on None in the gallery, which is the first selection and appears as a big X. The *Hot Tip* on page 161 indicates that cutting out elements from a photograph can also be done based on their color. PhotoDraw gives you the ability to identify different colors and cut out elements accordingly.

Cloning allows PhotoDraw learners to create an exact duplicate of an element in a photograph.

It is very important that learners understand the difference between the clone source and the clone destination. The ***clone source*** is what you want to clone or copy; the ***clone destination*** is the location where you want the copy to be placed. Click on **Touchup** and then on **Clone** to open the workpane and toolbar. Select the brush style you want to use by clicking on the arrow next to *Brush* on the workpane, to see the brush gallery. As you move the mouse pointer onto the workspace, it turns into a dashed shape that is the same as the selected brush shape. A small diamond appears inside the brush shape. Position the dashed shape on the element of the photograph that you want cloned, which is the clone source, and click the mouse button. The dashed shape will remain over this element. Now move the pointer to the location where you want the copy to be placed, which is the clone destination. A solid line in the shape of the brush will appear there. Click on the photograph where you want the clone to appear and the element will be copied there.

Cloning takes some practice and eye-hand coordination. Help learners acquire these skills by giving them time to clone the same image in a photograph and copy it elsewhere.

The Step-By-Step 10.2 activity clones one element from a photograph and places it in another location in that same photograph.

The *Note* concerning the second pointer that mimics the movement of your mouse can be a helpful tool. Once you have set your clone source, cloned the element, and moved it to your clone destination, any further movements of the clone source will likewise move the clone destination box in a parallel fashion. That is, if the clone source was originally one inch to the left of the clone destination, moving the clone source box will move the clone destination box in exactly the same way. Whenever you click the area now indicated by the clone source, it is copied to the clone destination. However, what if you want the original clone source to be copied? Then you must go back and reset the clone source in the toolbar. The *Hot Tip* shows that if you need to adjust the amount of transparency in an image you can move the *Amount* slider.

Hiding brings these various tools together to show how powerful PhotoDraw's photographic editing tools can be. One way to hide an element of a photograph is to place the clone of another element over it. Another way to hide an element of a photograph is to cut out a portion of one photograph and copy it onto another photograph. This second method is trickier because there has to be a close match between the elements and backgrounds of both photographs. Using the Edge slider here can be helpful. As with all PhotoDraw pictures, a photograph can be viewed in a Web browser.

The Step-By-Step 10.3 clones over one area of a photograph with another element of that same photograph to hide a window.

The year 1993, as the *Internet* tip on page 167 points out, was a watershed in terms of the Internet. Why was there a sudden explosion of Internet traffic? The next *Internet* tip gives the clear answer: the introduction of the browser Mosaic. Prior to this, lengthy commands had to be typed in if you wanted to visit another site or download a file. Spelling mistakes were common and this frustrated many users, discouraging them from trying to access the Web. With the introduction of the Web browser Mosaic, the Internet suddenly became a tool that anyone could use as long as they could click a mouse button. The *Hot Tip* on page 169 reveals a trick to use when cutting out and blending elements of one photograph with another. The background of a cut out element quite often will not perfectly match the background of the picture on which the cut out is to be pasted. To soften the edges of a cut out and help it to blend into its new location, click on **Edge** and then on **Soft Edges.**

Close

Have learners complete the end-of-lesson *Vocabulary Review* and *Review Questions. Vocabulary Review* requires learners to provide written definitions for key terms from the lesson. The *Review Questions* test learners' understanding of lesson concepts, requiring them to think critically about ideas discussed in class.

Project 10-1 directs learners to retrieve a photograph and crop out an element by shape.

Project 10-2 involves retrieving a PhotoDraw Content image and cloning a group of people. This is a good exercise for learners in using the clone tool because it demonstrates how powerful it can be. When finished, it is difficult to tell where the people were originally standing!

Project 10-3 asks the learners to retrieve two PhotoDraw Content images and hide an area by copying an element from one photograph into the other.

Critical Thinking has learners take pictures with a digital camera and correct them. As an option, you might want them to take pictures with a regular camera, have the pictures developed, and then stored on a photographic CD-ROM. Don't select the option of having the photographs stored on the Internet and then downloaded. Photographs developed and then stored for download are only in GIF format, while those on a CD-ROM are in JPEG format. These pictures are then to be touched up using the various PhotoDraw tools for photographic editing.

Assess

Assign the Lesson 10 Test located on the *Electronic Instructor* CD-ROM.

Vocabulary

cropping—Cutting out parts of a photograph

clipboard—A temporary holding area that can be accessed from any program designed to run on Microsoft Windows

cloning—Creating an exact duplicate

clone source—An element in a photograph that is copied or duplicated

clone destination—The final location of a cloned photographic element

SOLUTIONS FOR REVIEW QUESTIONS

PART B

LESSON 1 *Introduction to PhotoDraw*

TRUE/FALSE

T 1. Microsoft PhotoDraw 2000 Version 2 is a combination of several different application programs.

F 2. A completed design in PhotoDraw is called an object.

T 3. The workspace is the entire area that you use to create a picture.

T 4. The scratch area is the gray area that surrounds the background and serves as a temporary holding area.

F 5. Picture lists are at the right of the workspace and display the tools and options you need to perform a certain task.

FILL IN THE BLANK

1. The **menu bar** displays the names of the different menus.
2. The **standard toolbar** contains shortcut buttons or icons for commonly used menu commands.
3. The **visual** toolbar is really a combination of the menu bar and standard toolbar and is not found in other Microsoft Office applications.
4. Click on **Help** on the Standard toolbar and then **Contents and Index** to display the Help system.
5. When text is entered into a PhotoDraw picture those words form a(n) **text object**.

LESSON 2 *Using Templates and Wizards*

TRUE/FALSE

T 1. A template is a predefined PhotoDraw picture that is easy to modify.

T 2. When you first start PhotoDraw, the Microsoft PhotoDraw dialog box allows you to select a template.

F 3. Within each of the five major categories of templates there is only one subcategory.

F 4. The current active template subcategory is indicated by the red box surrounding it in the Picture List.

T 5. A tent card is folded in half and has a person's name or title printed on it.

F 6. Clicking the Cancel button while working on a template will close PhotoDraw.

T 7. You can move a text object by clicking on it and then dragging it to a new location in a template.

F 8. Print Report gives you the ability to print multiple pictures on one sheet of paper.

T 9. The Picture List displays thumbnails of all the pictures that are currently open in PhotoDraw.

T 10. A wizard asks a series of questions and then, based on your answers, it directs you through a sequence of steps to a completed project.

FILL IN THE BLANK

1. The **Save For Use In** wizard helps you save your PhotoDraw picture so that it can be used on the Web or in another Microsoft Office program.
2. Transporting a PhotoDraw picture to another Microsoft Office program, such as Word or PowerPoint, is known as **importing**.
3. The number of different template categories found in PhotoDraw is **5**.
4. The template category **Cards** can be used to create announcements, postcards, invitations, and tent cards.
5. When you start a template PhotoDraw will open the **Templates** workpane.

LESSON 3 *Creating a Web Page*

TRUE/FALSE

T 1. Web pages can be created in several different ways.

F 2. Hypertext Transport Protocol (HTTP) is the language that a Web browser program understands and translates into words and images to be viewed on a computer screen.

T 3. There are three basic steps in creating a Web page with PhotoDraw: Define the Web page, create the graphics and text, and preview and save the page.

T 4. Defining the Web page screen size involves determining the size of the page and creating its background.

T 5. Screen resolution is measured in the number of vertical and horizontal picture elements on a screen.

F 6. Most screen resolutions are set to 24 $\times$ 36 for creating Web pages.

F 7. PhotoDraw provides just one screen resolution to use when creating a Web page.

F 8. Most Web pages use a foreground image to attract attention.

F 9. To create a Web background by using templates, select **Templates** from the Visual Menu and then click on **Create.**

T 10. A transparent picture is one that looks faded because it allows a background color to "bleed" through it.

FILL IN THE BLANK

1. Microsoft includes a large number of PhotoDraw pictures that can be used and these pictures are called **PhotoDraw content** .
2. To make a picture transparent select **Transparency** from the **Effects** menu.
3. A transparency of **70** % is about right for a Web page background.
4. A(n) **banner** is a horizontal message that stretches across a page.
5. A(n) **hyperlink** is a connection that allows a web surfer to jump quickly from one Web page to another with a single click of the mouse button.

LESSON 4 *Using Draw*

TRUE/FALSE

F 1. Draw tools can create expressive freehand lines and shapes.

F 2. Use the Paint tools when you want to create precise shapes and have a fine degree of control over the image.

T 3. To draw a line, click the starting point of the line, drag to the ending point, and release the mouse button.

F 4. Scribble is used to draw an object with both curved and straight segments.

F 5. Freeform will create an object that looks like it was drawn freehand with a pen.

T 6. When drawing a curve, the mouse pointer will turn into a cross shape.

F 7. The last step in drawing a curve is to move the mouse to the point where you want the curve to end and single click.

T 8. The Freeform tool is a combination of the Line and Scribble tool.

F 9. To draw a freeform figure, drag the mouse pointer in the shape that you want and then release the mouse button.

T 10. Clicking on the Undo button will erase whatever you have just completed.

FILL IN THE BLANK

1. One way to correct mistakes made when drawing is to select the object and then press the **Delete** key.
2. Once you complete a drawing the icon button will "pop out", which is also known as **deselected**.
3. A(n) **shape** is a ready-made object, and includes lines, squares, circles, flowchart elements, and buttons.
4. To use an AutoShape, open the Draw Paint menu and then click on **AutoShapes**.
5. With **AutoShapes** you can drag one of the sizes of the selection box to reshape or distort the proportions of the shape.

LESSON 5 *Using Paint*

TRUE/FALSE

F 1. The PhotoDraw Paint tools let you create and edit very precise lines and shapes.

T 2. PhotoDraw divides its Paint tools into two categories: paintbrushes and other painting tools.

T 3. In the workpane gallery there are a wide variety of Paint tools from which to select, including *airbrush, pencil,* and *highlighter.*

F 4. A floating toolbar can be moved only to the Standard toolbar.

T 5. After creating an object, you can adjust the color by using the *Fill* visual menu option.

T 6. Because Paint is intended to produce freehand drawings, the line on the screen will look exactly as you created it.

F 7. Clip art are graphic images that you draw from scratch and can then be incorporated into PhotoDraw pictures.

T 8. As you paint using Photo Stamps, the stamps appear in random sizes and positions.

T 9. Artistic Brushes can create a picture that resembles what an artist would create using brushes or similar tools.

T 10. To modify the picture made with an artistic brush with another artistic brush style, click on the existing image in the workspace to select it and then click on the type of artistic brush style with which you want to replace it.

COMPLETION

1. A(n) **photo brush** creates a continuous unbroken line of a photographic image.
2. **Photo Stamps** are individual photographic images that can be repeated to form a line.
3. With **Paint** tools you can create expressive freehand lines and shapes but with **Draw** tools you create and edit very precise lines and shapes.
4. A toolbar that can be moved anywhere on the screen is called a(n) **floating** toolbar.
5. **Clip art** are graphic images that are already drawn and can be incorporated into PhotoDraw pictures.

LESSON 6 Opening, Inserting, and Saving Images

TRUE/FALSE

T 1. PhotoDraw uses a special file format called Microsoft Image Extension (MIX) when saving PhotoDraw files.

F 2. You can easily reopen a JPEG file and make changes to the objects.

F 3. PhotoDraw cannot open an image that has been saved in another file format other than MIX.

T 4. The GIF format can display a maximum of 256 colors of an image and is best for black-and-white line drawings, color clip art, and pictures that use large blocks of solid colors.

F 5. The JPEG format is new and is designed to replace GIF.

F 6. A file extension is a period followed by one letter in the file name that indicates what type of file it is.

T 7. To open a file, you can click on the *Open File* icon found on the standard toolbar.

T 8. By default, the *Files of type* is set to *All Supported Formats.*

F 9. You can select the specific file type (like *PhotoDraw 2000 (*.MIX))* that you're looking for by clicking on the down arrow next to *Open.*

T 10. *Open Read-Only* will open the file but you cannot make any changes to it.

FILL IN THE BLANK

1. **Visual Open** displays a thumbnail of the contents of each file and makes it very easy to locate the file you want to open quickly.
2. Unlike a traditional camera that records its images on film, a **digital** camera has no film.
3. **TWAIN (Technology Without An Interesting Name)** software drivers allows a digital camera to communicate with PhotoDraw and other programs.
4. All pictures created in PhotoDraw have a file extension of **MIX**, indicating that they are PhotoDraw graphic images.
5. To insert a graphic image directly from the Internet, click on the **File** menu and then click on **Open from Web Page.**

LESSON 7 *Arranging Objects*

TRUE/FALSE

T 1. Changing the size of an object is also known as resizing it.

F 2. To resize the object and maintain its proportions, drag a side size handle.

F 3. To distort the look of the object by stretching or squeezing it, drag a corner handle.

T 4. When you enter a number in the *Height* box on the *Arrange* workpane, PhotoDraw will automatically calculate a value for the *Width* box.

F 5. An object cannot be sized in one direction.

T 6. To resize an object so that it fits the workspace, select the object and then click on the **Crop Size** menu.

T 7. The option *Rotate Left* will move the object 90 degrees counter-clockwise, while *Rotate Right* will move it 90 degrees clockwise.

F 8. To mirror the position of the object, use *Flip Vertical.*

T 9. To make the object appear upside down, use *Flip Vertical.*

T 10. To align objects horizontally by their middles or vertically by their centers, select *Align Middle* or *Align Center.*

FILL IN THE BLANK

1. You can change the order of the foreground and background objects by using the *Order* commands on the **Arrange** menu.
2. To move the object forward by only one position, click on *Bring* **Forward**.
3. To move the object forward by only one position, click on *Send* **Backward**.
4. The **object** list displays objects that make up a picture along with the order of the objects.
5. To change an object's order, drag the object **downward** on the object list to move it to the background.

LESSON 8 *Special Effects*

TRUE/FALSE

T 1. To apply a shadow effect, first select the object on which you want the shadow to appear, then click on the **Effects** menu, and then on **Shadow** to display the *Shadow* workpane.

F 2. The *Shadow Transparency* option allows you to move the shadow by dragging it to a new position, enabling you to create the "time of day" you want the shadow to convey by lengthening the shadow or by shortening it.

F 3. To make a shadow more blurred, use the *Shadow Soften* option and set it to a lower number.

T 4. *Transparency* is a function that makes a picture look faded because it allows a background color to "bleed" through it.

T 5. *Transparency* makes the entire object look faded while Fade Out allows you to control the fading.

T 6. The *Transparency Start* slider lets you make the start of the fade more transparent while the *Transparency End* slider lets you make the end of the fade more transparent.

F 7. Colorizing an object means adding color to an object.

F 8. If you want your color to match identically with the colors found in other Microsoft Office products, click on the down arrow in the *True Color* line and select the Office product, like Word or FrontPage, that you want to match.

T 9. PhotoDraw has three palettes from which to choose.

T 10. The *True Color* tab will display the widest spectrum of color choices.

FILL IN THE BLANK

1. The opposite of colorizing is applying a(n) ______**negative**______ effect.
2. When using blur and sharpen, moving the slider to the ______**left**______ will blur the image.
3. To distort only a portion of the object, click on *Distort by* ______**painting**______.
4. The *Shadow* ______**Position**______ allows you to move the shadow by dragging it to a new position.
5. To use Fade Out, select the object and then click on ______**Effect**______ and then on *Fade Out.*

LESSON 9 *Retouching Photographs*

TRUE/FALSE

T 1. PhotoDraw provides special tools to correct the focus or the brightness of a photograph.

F 2. To sharpen a photograph, open the photograph in PhotoDraw and then click on **Touchup** and then on **Sharpen Photograph.**

T 3. Dragging the slider to the right or clicking on the up arrow will sharpen a photograph.

T 4. Brightness refers to how light or dark the object appears, while contrast refers to the difference between the lightest and darkest areas of the photograph.

F 5. There are three different ways in which you can adjust the brightness or contrast.

T 6. To make the object appear brighter, move the slider to the right in the *Brightness* setting, or to the left to make it darker.

T 7. If you shoot a photograph indoors without a flash, the resulting image might have an overall green or reddish tint.

F 8. When adjusting the tint, a window will open asking you to click on an area in the photograph that should be blue or light green.

F 9. The tint of a photograph cannot be adjusted manually.

F 10. To remove all of a color from a photograph, move the *Amount* slider to the right to remove the color.

FILL IN THE BLANK

1. The ____**hue**____ is the color of a color.
2. ____**Saturation**____ is the percentage of a particular hue present in a color.
3. The ____**color spectrum**____ is all the colors that the human eye can see.
4. ____**Red eye**____ occurs when the light from the flash reflects from the subject's retina back to the camera.
5. Dust on a camera lens will produce a photograph that has speckles called ____**dust spots**____.

LESSON 10 *Editing Photographs*

TRUE/FALSE

T 1. Retouching a photograph means to make "touch-up" improvements to it, while editing a photograph means to make radical changes to it, such as erasing portions of the photograph.

T 2. Cropping a photograph means to cut out unwanted portions of the image.

F 3. PhotoDraw provides tools to make six different types of crops on a photograph.

F 4. To erase part of a photograph and leave only a large white space in its place, click on **Crop Size** and then on **Delete.**

T 5. The **Edge** slider changes the edges of the area erased to hard (a sharp edge) or soft, (for blending into the photograph).

F 6. To keep one part of a photograph and erase everything else, click on **Crop Size** and then on **Crop.**

T 7. If you want to apply another crop to the same object, click on **Lock Crop** and then click on another shape.

T 8. To make a copy of part of a photograph and place it on the clipboard, click on **Crop Size** and then on **Cut Out.**

F 9. The clipboard is a temporary holding area that can be accessed only from Microsoft Office.

F 10. Click on **Edit** and then on **Copy** to copy from the clipboard to another program.

FILL IN THE BLANK

1. Click on ____**File**____ and then on **Preview in Browser** to start your computer's Web browser and view the Web page.
2. Use the ____**size**____ handles to increase or decrease the size of the element.
3. To place a cutout on the clipboard click on ____**Copy**____ on the floating toolbar.
4. The ____**clone source**____ is what you want to clone or copy.
5. The location of where you want the clone or copy to be placed is called the ____**clone destination**____.

PART C

PRINTED OUTPUTS FOR STEP-BY-STEP EXERCISES AND PROJECTS

The following pages contain printed outputs the learner is asked to produce during Step-by-Step exercises and projects. Learners' outputs may differ depending on the printer used and because some exercises allow the learner to choose his or her own preferences for style elements. Solution files that correspond to printed outputs are listed where applicable.

PRINTED OUTPUT FROM PROJECT 1-1

File Source: Project 1-1

Your Name
Your Address
City, State Zip Code

PhotoDraw Product Registration
1 Microsoft Way
Redmond, WA 99207

PRINTED OUTPUT FROM PROJECT 1-2
File Source: Project 1-2

Vena Stuart Elementary School

Announces the

Dedication

of our new building

780 HART STREET

Sunday, November 7

2:00- 4:00

The public is invited to attend

PRINTED OUTPUT FROM PROJECT 1-3
File Source: Project 1-3

Glamour Shots

Chdilren's Portrait Package

$59.95

Includes the following:
- 1 8x10
- 2 5x7
- 8 Wallets
- Photo Session

[illegible]

KIDS PIX PHOTOGRAPHERS
RIVERGATE MALL
888-0010

PRINTED OUTPUT FROM STEP-BY-STEP 2.2

File Source: Solution Step-by-Step 2-2

PRINTED OUTPUT FROM STEP-BY-STEP 2.3

File Source: Solution Step-by-Step 2-3

PRINTED OUTPUT FROM STEP-BY-STEP 2.4
File Source: Solution Step-by-Step 2-4

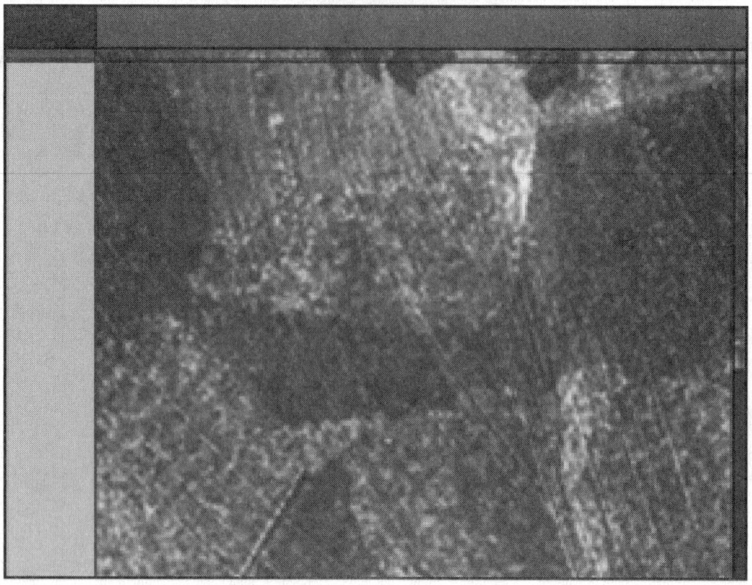

PRINTED OUTPUT FROM PROJECTS 2-1 AND 2-2
File Source: Project 2-1 and 2-2

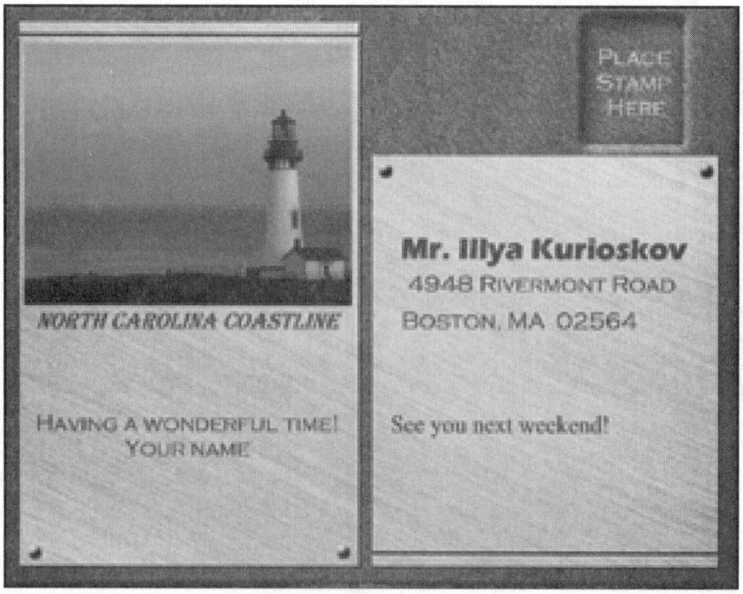

PRINTED OUTPUT FROM STEP-BY-STEP 3.3
File Source: Solution Step-by-Step 3-3

PRINTED OUTPUT FROM STEP-BY-STEP 3.4
File Source: Solution Step-by-Step 3-4

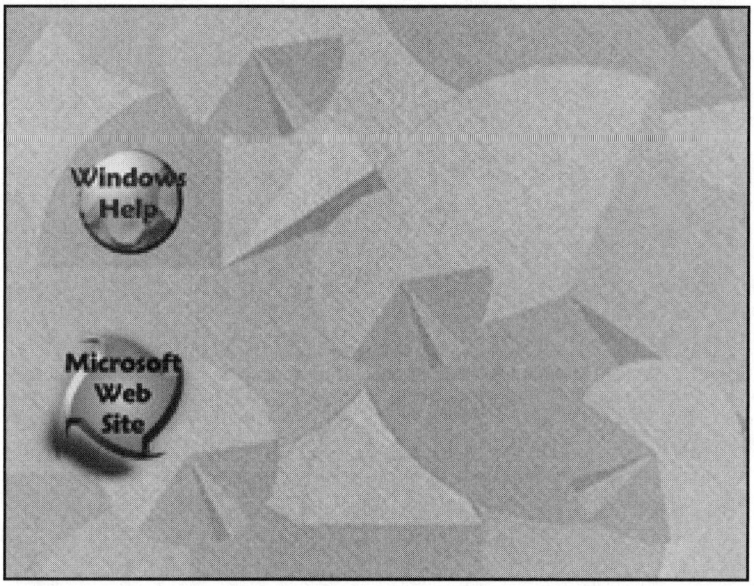

PRINTED OUTPUT FROM STEP-BY-STEP 3.5
File Source: Solution Step-by-Step 3-5

PRINTED OUTPUT FROM STEP-BY-STEP 3.6
File Source: Solution Step-by-Step 3-6

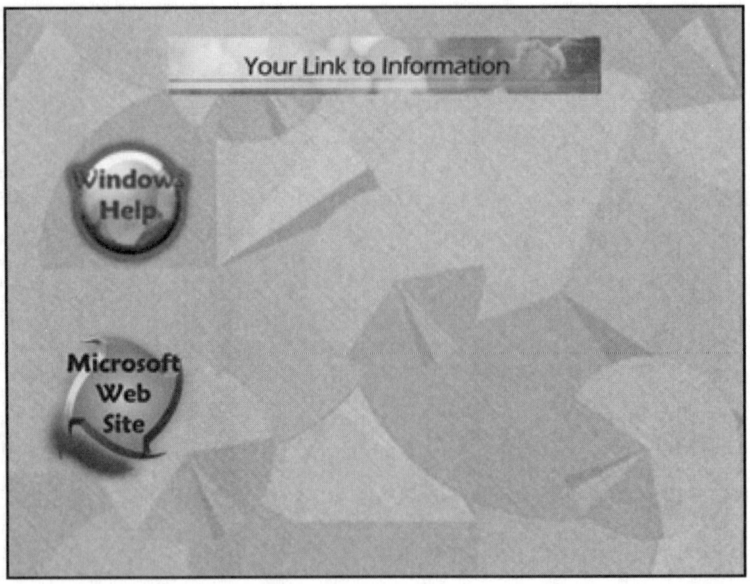

PRINTED OUTPUT FROM STEP-BY-STEP 3.7

File Source: Solution Step-by-Step 3-7

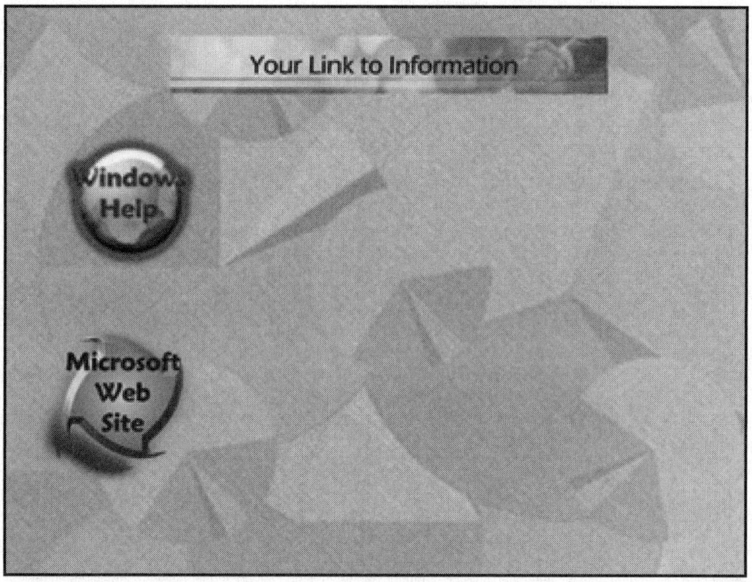

PRINTED OUTPUT FROM PROJECT 3-1

File Source: Project 3-1

PRINTED OUTPUT FROM PROJECT 3-2
File Source: Project 3-2

PRINTED OUTPUT FROM PROJECT 3-3
File Source: Project 3-3

PRINTED OUTPUT FROM STEP-BY-STEP 4.1

File Source: Solution Step-by-Step 4-1

PRINTED OUTPUT FROM STEP-BY-STEP 4.2
File Source: Solution Step-by-Step 4-2

Soccer & Stuff

PRINTED OUTPUT FROM STEP-BY-STEP 4.3

File Source: Solution Step-by-Step 4-3

Soccer & Stuff

PRINTED OUTPUT FROM PROJECT 4-1
File Source: Project 4-1

PRINTED OUTPUT FROM PROJECT 4-2
File Source: Project 4-2

PRINTED OUTPUT FROM PROJECT 4-3
File Source: Project 4-3

PRINTED OUTPUT FROM STEP-BY-STEP 5.1
File Source: Solution Step-by-Step 5-1

PRINTED OUTPUT FROM STEP-BY-STEP 5.2
File Source: Solution Step-by-Step 5-2

PRINTED OUTPUT FROM PROJECT 5-1
File Source: Project 5-1

PRINTED OUTPUT FROM PROJECT 5-2
File Source: Project 5-2

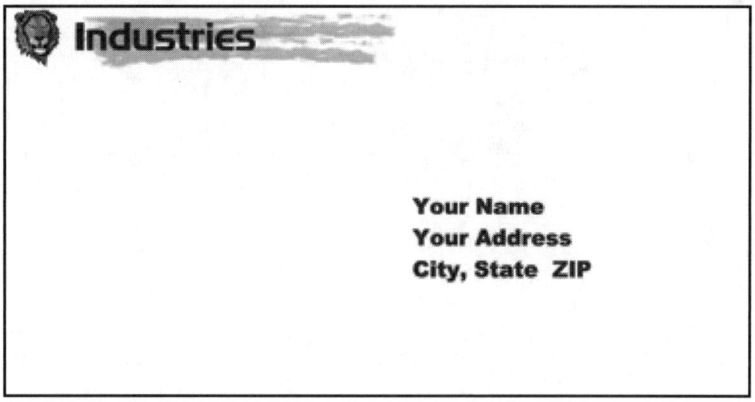

PRINTED OUTPUT FROM PROJECT 5-3
File Source: Project 5-3

PRINTED OUTPUT FROM STEP-BY-STEP 6.1A

File Source: Solution Step-by-Step 6-1A

PRINTED OUTPUT FROM STEP-BY-STEP 6.1B

File Source: Solution Step-by-Step 6-1B

PRINTED OUTPUT FROM STEP-BY-STEP 6.2

File Source: Solution Step-by-Step 6-2

PRINTED OUTPUT FROM PROJECT 6-1
File Source: Project 6-1

PRINTED OUTPUT FROM PROJECT 6-2
File Source: Project 6-2

PRINTED OUTPUT FROM PROJECT 6-3

File Source: Project 6-3

PRINTED OUTPUT FROM STEP-BY-STEP 7.2

File Source: Solution Step-by-Step 7-2

PRINTED OUTPUT FROM PROJECT 7-1
File Source: Project 7-1

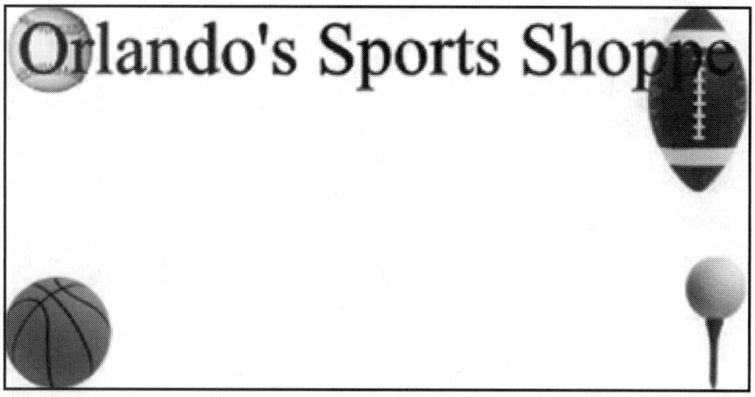

PRINTED OUTPUT FROM PROJECT 7-2
File Source: Project 7-2

PRINTED OUTPUT FROM PROJECT 7-3
File Source: Project 7-3

PRINTED OUTPUT FROM STEP-BY-STEP 8.1
File Source: Solution Step-by-Step 8-1

PRINTED OUTPUT FROM STEP-BY-STEP 8.2

File Source: Solution Step-by-Step 8-2

Caution!

Step

Down

PRINTED OUTPUT FROM STEP-BY-STEP 8.3

File Source: Solution Step-by-Step 8-3

PRINTED OUTPUT FROM PROJECT 8-1

File Source: Project 8-1

PRINTED OUTPUT FROM PROJECT 8-2

File Source: Project 8-2

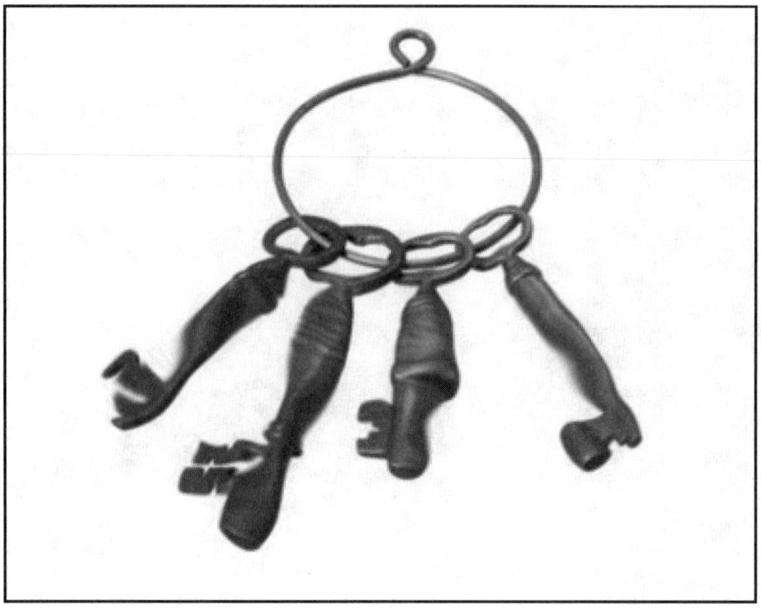

PRINTED OUTPUT FROM PROJECT 8-3

File Source: Project 8-3

PRINTED OUTPUT FROM STEP-BY-STEP 9.1

File Source: Solution Step-by-Step 9-1

PRINTED OUTPUT FROM STEP-BY-STEP 9.2

File Source: Solution Step-by-Step 9-2

PRINTED OUTPUT FROM STEP-BY-STEP 9.3

File Source: Solution Step-by-Step 9-3

PRINTED OUTPUT FROM PROJECT 9-1

File Source: Project 9-1

PRINTED OUTPUT FROM PROJECT 9-2

File Source: Project 9-2

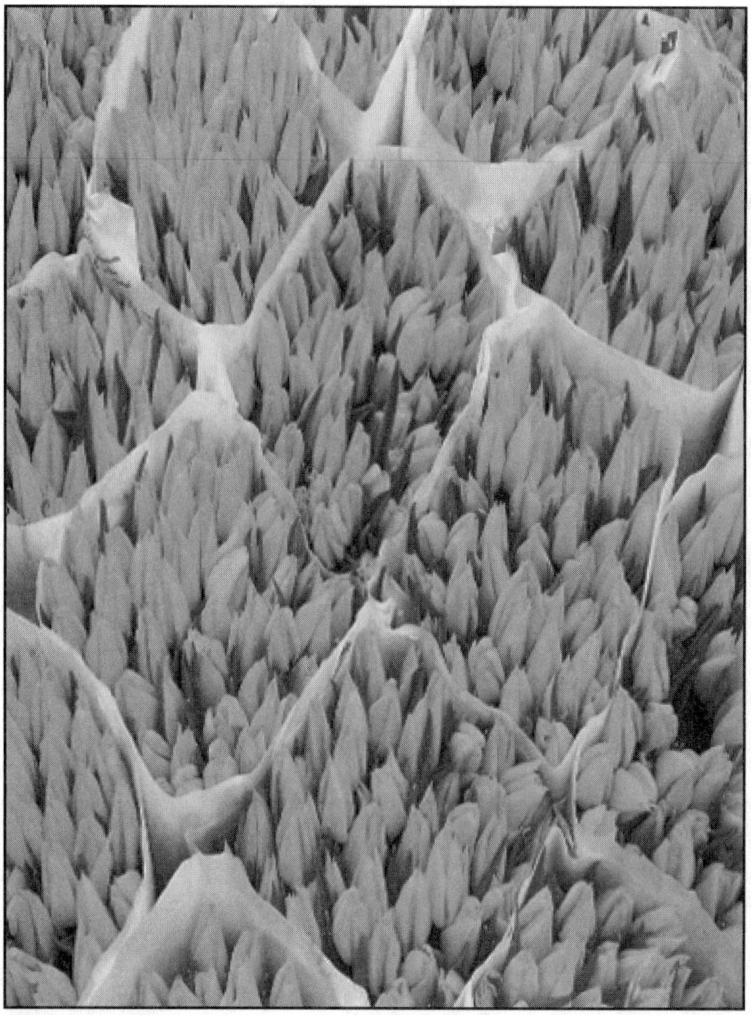

PRINTED OUTPUT FROM PROJECT 9-3
File Source: Project 9-3

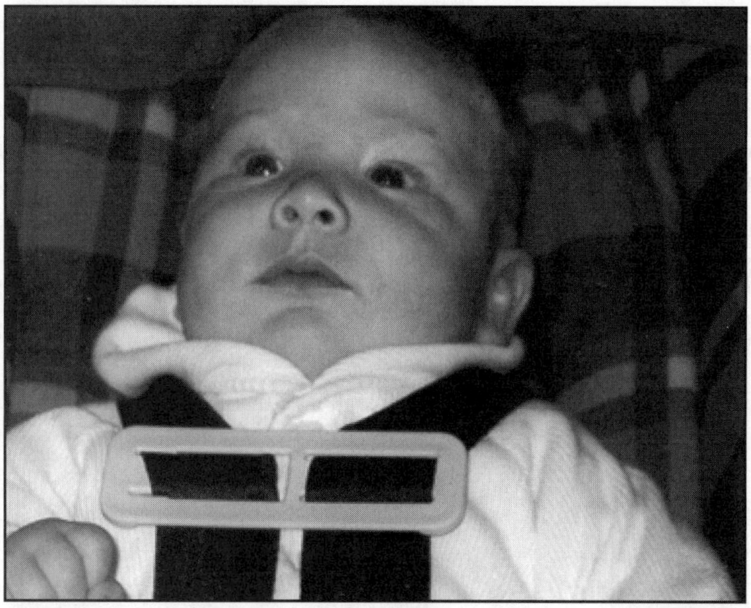

PRINTED OUTPUT FROM STEP-BY-STEP 10.1
File Source: Solution Step-by-Step 10-1

PRINTED OUTPUT FROM STEP-BY-STEP 10.2

File Source: Solution Step-by-Step 10-2

PRINTED OUTPUT FROM STEP-BY-STEP 10.3

File Source: Solution Step-by-Step 10-3

PRINTED OUTPUT FROM PROJECT 10-1

File Source: Project 10-1

PRINTED OUTPUT FROM PROJECT 10-2

File Source: Project 10-2

PRINTED OUTPUT FROM PROJECT 10-3

File Source: Project 10-3